L.A. STORY

Shohei Ohtani, the Los Angeles Dodgers, and a Season for the Ages

Bill Plunkett

TRIUMPH
BOOKS

Library of Congress Cataloging-in-Publication Data is available upon request

This book is available in quantity at special discounts for your group or organization. For further information, contact:

Triumph Books LLC
814 North Franklin
Chicago, Illinois 60610
(312) 337-0747
www.triumphbooks.com

Printed in U.S.A.
ISBN 978-1-63727-765-2
Design by Patricia Frey

To Janis, the best wife a ballwriter could ever have. She's my lobster.

Contents

"Wan-chan genki?"

From their earliest days playing in the shadow of the Hollywood sign, the Los Angeles Dodgers have had their share of stars.

From Sandy Koufax and Don Drysdale in the 1960s to Steve Garvey in the '70s, Fernando Valenzuela and Kirk Gibson in the '80s, Mike Piazza in the '90s, Clayton Kershaw in the 2000s, and even the brief but exciting "Wild Horse" days of Yasiel Puig. Their long-time broadcaster, Vin Scully, grew to legendary status as well, hailed as the greatest play-by-play man in baseball if not sports history.

The Dodgers' manager even became a star.

Over his 21 seasons in the dugout at Dodger Stadium, Tommy Lasorda hobnobbed with celebrities until he became one himself. Friends with stars including Frank Sinatra and comedian Don Rickles, Lasorda became a frequent guest on television talk shows—and an even more frequent target of those same TV hosts who poked fun at Lasorda's love of Italian food, his ample belly, and his failed attempts to control it, even as he shilled for the SlimFast diet plan in oft-mocked commercials.

Lasorda used his celebrity to spread the gospel of Dodgers baseball, claiming to bleed Dodger blue and calling Dodger Stadium "Blue Heaven on Earth."

"If you want to go to heaven, you have to go through Dodger Stadium first," Lasorda once claimed.

Has any other franchise been ground zero for not one but two "Manias"—Fernandomania and Nomomania?

Valenzuela burst onto the scene in 1981, an unknown 20-year-old from a small town in Mexico who seemed to roll his eyes toward heaven with every delivery while baffling major-league hitters. Every Fernando start was an event, drawing sold-out crowds and bringing a new segment of fans to the Dodgers on his way to winning both the Rookie of the Year and Cy Young awards.

Fourteen years later, Hideo Nomo arrived in Los Angeles, an unknown commodity in his own right. Though Nomo had already forged a successful career in Japan, no one knew how that would translate to Major League Baseball. It hadn't been done before. Nomo was a pioneer for the numerous Japanese stars who would follow, making the All-Star team and also winning the Rookie of the Year Award.

Like Valenzuela, Nomo mesmerized with a unique delivery that prompted the nickname "The Tornado" and drew a new segment of fans to the Dodgers' following.

But Shohei Ohtani's decision to join the Dodgers was different.

Unlike Valenzuela or Nomo, Ohtani joined the Dodgers as very much a known commodity—one with two American League Most Valuable Player Awards already under his belt. A two-way player in a sport that had evolved toward specialization, Ohtani was already a unique attraction that made him one of the faces of his sport.

Baseball has never seen a player like Shohei Ohtani. That much was obvious during his first six seasons in Major League Baseball as Ohtani established his one-of-a-kind ability to be both one of the best hitters in baseball and an elite pitcher. It's something the sport has not seen since the early years of Babe Ruth's career over a century ago—and has never seen to the level at which Ohtani has performed. Professional sports as a whole have seen very few athletes rise to the level of global celebrity with the impact, economic power, and draw that Ohtani has achieved. His move to the Dodgers only heightened that celebrity and drawing power. The global brand of Ohtani in the prime of his career has combined with the legacy brand of the Dodgers, one of MLB's crown-jewel franchises located in the large, star-obsessed, Hollywood-flavored market of Southern California.

"You might have played with other teams—that's the big leagues," the Hall of Famer Lasorda used to say about his beloved franchise. "But when you come to the Dodgers, it's the *major* leagues."

The mass media attention that the marriage of Ohtani and the Dodgers would bring was evident from the start.

The press conference to introduce Ohtani as a Dodger, held in the center-field plaza at Dodger Stadium shortly after his signing in December 2023, attracted approximately 300 reporters, camera operators, and photographers. It was televised by SportsNet LA (the Dodgers' broadcast network), NHK in Japan, MLB Network, and on the ESPN app, as well as YouTube.

"No player moves the needle in baseball more than Shohei, as far as on a global scale," Dodgers manager Dave Roberts said later.

When Ohtani reported to the Dodgers' Camelback Ranch training complex in Arizona in early February—days before pitchers and catchers were scheduled to report—the Japanese media was there to meet him. A few dozen camera operators lined up at 6:00 AM each day just to capture video of Ohtani driving into the parking lot outside the main building. One morning, one enterprising camera operator even stationed himself at the intersection where Ohtani would turn onto the road to the complex.

"These guys are like Taylor Swift in Japan," veteran pitcher Clayton Kershaw said of Ohtani and the team's other signing from Japan, pitcher Yoshinobu Yamamoto. "We become a bigger deal because we're associated with them. It just means there's a lot more eyes on us from different parts of the world—which is cool."

Most springs there are just four sources that cover spring training on a daily basis for the entirety of the Dodgers' stay in Arizona—the *Los Angeles Times*, The Athletic, MLB.com, and me, providing coverage to the 12 newspapers of the Southern California Newspaper Group (including the *Orange County Register* and *Los Angeles Daily News*). SportsNet LA also provides daily coverage throughout spring training. Reporters and columnists from national outlets like ESPN, *USA Today*, *Sports Illustrated*, Fox, and Yahoo! Sports, as well as others, make occasional visits to write feature stories and columns. But there are rarely more than 10 or 12 reporters on any given day.

That all changed with Ohtani's arrival in 2024.

Applications for daily credentials to cover spring training nearly doubled from 2023. The media workroom inside the main building at Camelback Ranch could only accommodate about a dozen reporters, so the Dodgers set up a large tent in the parking lot for the overflow. The venue—complete with flat-screen TVs and a cooler filled with soft drinks—was dubbed "The White House" by the reporters who made it their work home for five weeks of spring training.

"I think baseball is kind of covered differently than other sports, and when you get kind of the personalities and the following that those two guys [Ohtani and Yamamoto] get, it kind of becomes a little more like a football Sunday every day," Dodgers pitcher Walker Buehler said. "You can kind of go back to the World Baseball Classic [in 2023] and the coverage and the energy and the vibe that that gets. I think it's good for the game to be covered in this way. We're fortunate to have it here."

The Dodger players did not always feel "fortunate" when they saw the larger numbers of reporters invading the clubhouse on a daily basis. In fact, Dodgers PR put some restrictions on clubhouse access during spring training when the number of cameras, in particular, became unwieldy.

"When we drive in, there's about 30 people [media] outside our parking lot. That wasn't there the last couple years. Yeah, we notice it," Dodgers first baseman Freddie Freeman said of the extra attention drawn by Ohtani and Yamamoto in the spring. "But I think it's more of—that's a good thing. That means good things happened this off-season for the Dodgers. We've got…probably the guy we're going to be talking about to our great-grandchildren. Just like we talk about Babe Ruth, we're going to talk about Shohei. It's just an exciting time for the Dodgers, for us."

When Ohtani purchased a home in the Los Angeles area early in the season, that attention crossed a line, and some members of the media went too far.

In late May, Ohtani completed the purchase of a mansion formerly owned by comedian Adam Carolla, paying $7.85 million for the property in La Cañada Flintridge, about a dozen miles from Dodger Stadium. The three-story home came complete with five bedrooms, six and a half bathrooms, a movie theater, sauna, gym, and basketball court.

But the location of Ohtani's new home became public knowledge, and TV crews from Fuji TV and Nippon TV descended on the neighborhood, taking shots of the exterior and setting up their cameras to interview neighbors.

Celebrities in the L.A. area—including Dodger players—have been victimized by home break-ins frequently in recent years, heightening concerns over security. The TV crews crossed a line in the view of the Dodgers, and their credentials to cover games at Dodger Stadium were revoked.

Concerns about security and a lack of privacy prompted Ohtani and his wife to delay moving into their new home, and they eventually put it up for sale in July without ever spending a night there.

"I can't put myself in those shoes—just how much he has to go through, people wanting to know where he lives and all that stuff," Freeman said. "And he's still a joy for us in the clubhouse.

"I just can't even imagine what he goes through on a day to day."

The experience led to a chilling of Ohtani's relationship with the media. During his final season with the Los Angeles Angels, Ohtani granted interviews only on days when he pitched, then disappeared entirely after he suffered an injury.

Ohtani was more accessible during the first months of his debut season with the Dodgers. But it quickly became protocol that all requests had to go through the Dodgers' media relations staff—and if the interview occurred, it had to happen in front of a special backdrop featuring the logos of Japanese sponsors (All Nippon Airways, Toyo Tires, and Daiso, alongside Guggenheim and the Dodgers). The same backdrop was used whenever Yamamoto talked with the media.

Already problematic for reporters seeking access to the star, Ohtani stopped doing pregame interviews entirely as the season progressed (after doing them only occasionally in the first half of the season). Media members covering the team protested against the mandate demanded by Ohtani's agent, Nez Balelo, to no avail.

For Dave Roberts, the added media attention and fan demands on a daily basis "had to be part of the calculus" for Dodger players preparing for the 2024 season.

"To have two marquee Japanese ballplayers playing for the Dodgers sort of goes back to where Hideo Nomo came over. For us as an organization, to see Dodger uniforms all over the country and all over Asia is something that excites us all," Roberts said.

"I do think that when you put this uniform on, there's a certain standard in how you go about things. Appreciating the fact that there's more responsibility, more autographs to sign, more media probably to contend with and stuff out in the community. Then obviously on the field, [there are] expectations. I think all that—I don't know if we're prepared for it. I think that we're going to learn as we go. But I think that's what we're in store for."

Roberts said there would be "a learning curve for everyone" and his message to his team would be to embrace the opportunity and expectations that come with playing for a high-profile franchise like the Dodgers.

Could all the media attention be a distraction, though?

"If you let it," he said. "But I think if you go in appreciating this opportunity to get in front of people, that's part of playing for the Dodgers. So I think that, yeah, it can be a distraction. But I don't think it will be for our club."

During more than 20 years as a baseball beat writer, reporting daily at various times on the Angels and Dodgers, I have covered a long list of Japanese players—from Hideo Nomo, Takashi Saito, Kaz Ishii, and Kenta Maeda with the Dodgers to Shigetoshi Hasegawa, Hisanori Takahashi, and Hideki Matsui during my years on the Angels beat. So I was prepared for an influx of Japanese media to follow Ohtani north up the 5 Freeway from Anaheim to Los Angeles.

But none of those players drew the attention that Ohtani does. Only Nomo in his early days or Matsui even came close.

When Matsui joined the Angels in 2010, he had just won the World Series MVP award with the champion New York Yankees in 2009. A contingent of a couple dozen Japanese reporters came with him.

Matsui handled the attention remarkably well. Reporters would line up in front of his locker daily to get a minute or two of his time. He would accommodate everyone.

When the season ended—and the Angels did not make the playoffs—we all got together to play softball at Angel Stadium. It was an international friendly in soccer terms—the Japanese media vs. the American reporters and members of the Angels' front office.

Matsui showed up and played with us. The left-handed outfielder batted right-handed and played on the American team. Afterwards, he stayed and posed for photos with each of the Japanese reporters and their families.

Those of us who cover baseball on a daily basis spend a good deal of time standing around and waiting—outside clubhouses, inside clubhouses, in dugouts, etc. That time has allowed me to make friends with a number of Japanese reporters over the years—people like Sam Onoda (a freelance producer who works for NHK and has covered Ichiro Suzuki, Kenta Maeda, and Matsui, as well as Ohtani); Takako Nakamichi (another TV journalist); Hideki Okuda, who writes for *Sports Nippon*; Masa Niwa of *Sankei Sports*; and Taro Abe, who writes for *Chunichi Shimbun*.

Spending so much time together, I have learned some Japanese words and phrases from them and often used them with the players—to the amusement of the players and reporters alike. It's a way to make them relax, and for me to stand out from the media crowd and build relationships.

The rules for covering Shohei Ohtani quickly became evident during the early days of spring training:

Rule One: if Ohtani does something, it's news.

Rule Two: if Ohtani *doesn't* do something, that's news too.

Ohtani arrived at Camelback Ranch five months removed from his second reconstructive elbow surgery. The Dodgers had already ruled out him pitching until 2025, but Ohtani was aiming to complete his rehab from the surgery and be ready to serve as the Dodgers' designated hitter from the early start of the season, when the Dodgers would play two historic games in Seoul, South Korea.

Covering his rehab was difficult early in spring training because most of it went on behind the scenes in the large facility known as "The Lab," which contained batting cages and high-tech virtual reality technology for hitters to use.

Ohtani was expected to start taking batting practice on the field at some point. Soon, his name appeared on the list of hitters scheduled for on-field batting practice posted in the Dodgers' locker room and visible to the media. But Ohtani never appeared on the field to take batting practice.

Consult Rule Two of covering Ohtani: if Ohtani doesn't do something, that's news.

Ohtani speaks to the media infrequently—a stance that became a bone of contention between the media and the Dodgers frequently throughout the season—and he wasn't available to explain why he hadn't hit on the field one particular day.

After the workout when the clubhouse opened to the media, I was walking around a corner of the building heading to the clubhouse entrance. Out of the clubhouse and heading toward me came Ohtani with his then interpreter, Ippei Mizuhara, and a number of Japanese reporters.

One of the mysteries of Ohtani's free agency was the identity of the dog who appeared with him during the announcement of his second MVP, in November 2023. For weeks, no one knew the dog's name. So I learned how to ask the obvious question in Japanese—*"Wan-chan no namae nanni?"* in hope of solving the mystery.

By the time I got a chance to ask Ohtani, the dog's name— *Dekopin*, or Decoy—had come to light.

But as he walked away from the clubhouse door that day, I said, *"Wan-chan genki?"*—another phrase I had learned from my Japanese friends.

Ohtani stopped in his tracks, looked at me, and said Dekopin was fine—and that my Japanese was good. I thanked him— *"Arigato"*—and used the opening to ask about his not taking batting practice on the field yet. He explained that his name was on the list in case he decided to join a group on the field, but he didn't expect to progress to that point until the following week.

It was a small news item for me—but a big story for the Japanese reporters who saw the exchange.

I wound up doing more interviews that day than Ohtani, explaining how I had learned my Japanese and what I thought about covering him. A story including a photo—my face surrounded by Japanese characters—even appeared on the first page of *Sports Nippon* the next day.

I joked with the Japanese reporters that I wanted to build my brand in Japan as the "*Wan-chan Genki* Guy" and suggested that Ohtani and I should re-enact the encounter as a dog food commercial. At the very least, I might be able to score some free dog food for my own *wan-chan*.

It was the first but not the last time I would draw media coverage for my Japanese interactions with Ohtani.

But it was an early lesson on just how different things would be covering the Dodgers and Ohtani during a historic season in 2024.

Chapter 1

White Whale

As the most unique free agency in his sport's history played out—one that resulted in Shohei Ohtani signing the most lucrative contract in sports history with the Los Angeles Dodgers in December 2023—it was suggested that Ohtani was Andrew Friedman's "white whale," a one-of-a-kind player with whom Friedman had become obsessed.

Friedman does not appreciate the analogy and won't engage with the suggestion. Instead, he acknowledges being "intrigued" with Ohtani as far back as October 2012, when Friedman was GM of the Tampa Bay Rays and a teenaged Ohtani announced his intention to go from high school to a major-league organization in the United States.

There was little chance Friedman's Rays would be able to convince Ohtani to skip professional baseball in Japan and join them. There was, however, a very real possibility Ohtani would take his talents to a big-market, big-money franchise like the Dodgers.

Thus began a decade-long, on-again, off-again romance between Ohtani and the Dodgers.

The initial flirtation didn't last long. A handful of MLB organizations were interested in signing Ohtani directly out of high school. The Dodgers were considered the favorites in a group that also included the Boston Red Sox, the New York Yankees, and the Texas Rangers. The Dodgers viewed the high school star as an elite pitching prospect. As an 18-year-old, Ohtani had thrown a fastball recorded at 99 mph during the national high school championship tournament—the popular "Summer Kōshien." But even with that precocious talent, in the Dodgers' eyes, Ohtani would need time in the minor leagues before he would be ready to compete in MLB.

"We knew it was going to be a long shot, thinking he'd want to begin his professional career at home," reflected Ned Colletti, then the Dodgers GM.

Despite the MLB interest—and Ohtani's own expressed interest in jumping to MLB—the Nippon Ham Fighters chose Ohtani in the first round of the NPB draft and used both of those factors to woo him.

The Fighters warned him about the challenges of minor-league life in small-town America, showing him a video illustrating the hardships. And they told him he could pursue his dream of being a two-way player for them in the NPB. A jump to MLB someday was inevitable, the Fighters knew. But they told Ohtani he could establish his two-way talents while starring in Japan first.

And so he did.

He was an NPB All-Star as a rookie, reached double digits in wins and home runs in his second season, and threw a 101-mph pitch during the 2014 NPB All-Star Game and again during a regular-season game later that year. In 2016, he was the Pacific League's Most Valuable Player, leading the Fighters to the Japan Series championship.

Ohtani missed the 2017 World Baseball Classic due to an ankle injury that required surgery following the season. But he decided it was time to make the jump to the major leagues—despite international signing rules that would limit the bonus he could be offered by MLB teams.

The romance was renewed.

Friedman, by then the Dodgers' president of baseball operations, said only at that time that Ohtani's potential availability was "a situation that we are monitoring closely."

The Dodgers had been monitoring it for some time by then. In fact, in August 2017, Friedman, along with director of player personnel Galen Carr and former Dodgers pitcher (now broadcaster) Orel Hershiser, was spotted watching Ohtani throw a bullpen session and play a game for the Fighters.

As a scout with the Boston Red Sox before joining the Dodgers' front office under Friedman, Carr had been scouting Ohtani for years by then.

"I don't think there's anything special about saying this. I really don't," Carr reflected during the 2024 season. "I was over in Japan a bunch. A lot of other people came over to look at him. For my money, I'd never seen this combination of tools, of talent, ever. So it wasn't a big leap to say he has a chance to be a Hall of Famer.

"We put grades on guys. It's 2 to 8. Eight is a Hall of Famer. That's the grade we gave him before he came over from Japan.

Maybe a 7 as a hitter. You were seeing some contact-ability. You were seeing tremendous power…. This guy was throwing 100 [mph]. He's got an 80 [grade] split. He's got 80 power. He puts the ball in play and he runs like a 3.9 down the line. What is this? Where was this manufactured?

"From a collection-of-tools standpoint, it was unprecedented in our baseball lifetimes, certainly mine."

Carr recalled one moment during one of his 2017 visits that stood out and taught him something about how driven Ohtani was.

"I remember he had hurt his ankle and was on a minor-league rehab," Carr said. "Nippon Ham's minor-league facility was fairly close to Tokyo, so of course he was playing in a game there and it was packed. I went three days in a row to see him work out. Nobody in the stadium. This was a guy who would just work on his craft.

"He took about 100 swings in BP [batting practice]. Like 90 of them he's literally carving the ball down the left-field line—trying to let the ball get deep, staying inside of it, really focused on work. Maybe the last eight or 10 swings, he just unleashes and hits the ball 500 feet.

"The focus and the intent—he's not just, 'I'm going to work on hitting it further than I can already hit it.'"

With the help of his agent, Nez Balelo, Ohtani took the same focused approach to choosing his MLB team. Because he was still under 25 years old, Ohtani was only eligible for a minimal signing bonus, so Balelo sent all 30 MLB teams a questionnaire, seeking to distinguish teams in other ways.

Dodgers team president and CEO Stan Kasten has been involved in high-stakes free agency situations in multiple sports. Kasten was GM of the Atlanta Hawks in the NBA and president of the Atlanta Thrashers in the NHL, as well as president of the Atlanta Braves and Washington Nationals before joining the Dodgers when Guggenheim Baseball Management purchased the team in 2012.

Ohtani's free agency was "different" than most, even the first time around in 2017.

"There was a cutdown to six or seven teams that made the cut to have personal interviews," Kasten recalled in 2024. "A fair amount of cloak-and-dagger."

The Dodgers—coming off a World Series appearance in October 2017—had several advantages over the other contenders, including geography, a large Japanese American community in Los Angeles, a history with Japanese players, a sophisticated and forward-thinking front office, and a strong player development system.

They had one big handicap, however. The National League had not yet adopted the designated hitter rule, limiting Ohtani's ability to hit when he wasn't pitching.

"We definitely think that it's doable for someone who's talented enough to do both," Friedman said in the winter of 2017. "It takes being a little creative and trying to figure out the schedule and figure out recovery days. But we definitely think it's doable, and if we were ever to sign a player who's talented enough to do both, we'd look forward to the challenge of being creative to figure that out."

In retrospect, Friedman still calls that "a challenge" the Dodgers tried hard to address during their presentation to Ohtani and Balelo. When a list of seven finalists was reported, the Dodgers were on it and got one of the limited opportunities to make their pitch in person to Ohtani.

Not surprisingly, so were four other West Coast teams—the Angels, San Diego Padres, San Francisco Giants, and Seattle Mariners. Surprisingly, though, the list did include four National League teams—the Dodgers, Padres, Giants, and Chicago Cubs.

In the end, Ohtani surprised many in the baseball world by choosing to sign with the Angels, the franchise often buried in the Dodgers' shadow. In the end, the NL's lack of a DH was too much for the Dodgers to overcome.

"I was. But I kind of understood it," Galen Carr said of being surprised by Ohtani's choice. "We had really worked hard to come up with a plan where he could pitch and hit. But it was, 'Okay, you'll start as a DH in AL parks. You'll pinch-hit regularly.' I think we got close to 300 plate appearances in that mockup. I understood it [Ohtani's decision].

"We felt like if we had the DH at that time he would have been a Dodger. That's how we felt. We never knew for sure. I don't think we've asked him. We should someday."

Kasten has never asked Ohtani if he would have signed with the Dodgers, had DH been an option. But the team president referred to the Dodgers' first two swings-and-misses at signing Ohtani during the 2023 courtship.

"I did say during our process when he came here [to visit in December 2023] and was going through the process, 'Ten years ago, six years ago—things would have been really different if you had signed here. Don't make the same mistake,'" Kasten said. "That made him crack up. We all cracked up.

"I don't know what would have happened [if the National League had the DH rule in 2018]. I really don't. But there's always been such a logic to being with the Dodgers—I said that all winter."

In hindsight, Friedman is not sure the Dodgers' efforts were doomed from the start.

"I can't answer that. I'm not sure," he said in 2024. "But we knew it would be a challenge and we tried to address it as much as we could in our presentation. We spent a lot of time selling the Los Angeles area and how we would use him. I remember 15 seconds after it came out that he had chosen the Angels, my brother sent me a text saying, 'Hey—great job selling the L.A. area.'"

Infielders Justin Turner and Chris Taylor, as well as pitcher Clayton Kershaw, had less of a sense of humor about the recruiting efforts.

The three were enlisted by the Dodgers' front office to try and woo Ohtani. Turner was preparing for his wedding that winter. Kershaw flew from Texas to L.A. on his own wedding anniversary.

"I felt like it was a waste of time," Turner told the *Los Angeles Times* the next spring.

Kershaw topped that.

"Just a gigantic waste of time," he said.

"It really just seemed like it was predetermined that he wanted to DH. I'm kind of mad at his agent for making us waste all that time and effort. Fifteen teams [the National League teams] should have been out of it from the beginning."

Six years later, after spending most of a season as Ohtani's teammate in Dodger blue, Kershaw still felt it had been a "gigantic waste of time."

"Yeah, it was," Kershaw said late in the 2024 season. "Because he was going to DH. We didn't have the DH [in the National League]. I don't know if that was our front office 'pie in the sky' or his agent trying to leverage the Dodgers [to get more from another team] or whatever. I wasn't mad at Shohei. Shohei was just doing what he had to do. Either his agent was playing the game—either our side or his side shouldn't have flown us out. Because there was no way. There's nothing we could have said. Obviously, he was a pretty good hitter, so he's going to DH."

And so it was that the legend of Ohtani was set to blossom 35 miles south of Dodger Stadium in the very different atmosphere of Orange County.

While the Dodgers made the playoffs each year and returned to the World Series twice (winning in the pandemic bubble of 2020), Ohtani spent six seasons in relative obscurity as an Angel, achieving individual success (a Rookie of the Year Award in 2018, American League MVPs in 2021 and 2023) and establishing himself as a 21st century Babe Ruth—but never coming anywhere near the postseason. The Angels finished fourth in the five-team American League West five times in Ohtani's six seasons with them, and in third place in the sixth.

It was a very different atmosphere with a far different set of expectations than Ohtani would have experienced if he had signed with the Dodgers in 2018.

"I would have loved to have run that scenario out," Dodgers manager Dave Roberts said in 2024 when asked if he ever let himself wonder how things might have played out if Ohtani had chosen the Dodgers originally. "I think we had the personnel, the infrastructure to make it work. It would certainly have taken buy-in from players—which I would expect they would have done. But I do understand and appreciate the fact that—I don't want to say it with any disrespect [to the Angels] but a softer landing could have been beneficial for Shohei. But I also believe that if he would have signed with us out of the get-go, he would have flourished with us his first year."

The Angels' inability to build a contender—and All-Star Mike Trout's inability to stay healthy and team with Ohtani—led to speculation that the team would eventually trade Ohtani elsewhere in exchange for a franchise-altering package of prospects.

Ohtani's value as a marketing tool and the Angels' own dysfunction never made that more than speculation. Instead, Ohtani headed toward free agency following his second MVP season.

And the Dodgers once again leapt to the head of the class of potential suitors.

In fact, in some ways, it seemed inevitable that Ohtani would finally end up in Dodger blue.

"I guess," Galen Carr said to that perception. "You never want to take stuff like that for granted. But all the boxes seemed to be checked as far as it being a great destination for him. I feel like so much of that has to do with Los Angeles. It's Southern California. It's Los Angeles. The diversity of the city. How can that not appeal?"

Kasten felt even more strongly that a marriage between Shohei Ohtani and the Dodgers—even if delayed—made more sense than any other pairing.

"It was proximity. It was the history. It was prospective view of the franchise. It was facilities. It was all of that," Kasten said. "We were the only ones who made sense. I always felt that way. It doesn't always rule the day. But I always felt the logic was here."

And this time around, the Dodgers' financial resources would come into play. There would be no restrictions on what Ohtani could sign for, and estimates quickly escalated to $500 million.

Brandon Gomes was in the Dodgers' player development department during the 2017 pursuit of Ohtani. This time around, he would be in the thick of it as the Dodgers' general manager.

"I wasn't part of the first go-round," Gomes said in 2024. "Obviously things evolve. Priorities change. With Shohei, there just wasn't a whole lot of public information. He's a very private guy. So it was, okay, [let's emphasize] what we were able to provide as far as winning and culture and the commitment to be good now and in the future.

"From everything we had heard, that is what was important to him. We felt like we were in a good place on that front. Then it was just about personalized touches."

That signing Ohtani was important to the Dodgers seemed obvious if one looked at the character of their off-season after the 2022 season. They let popular players Justin Turner and Cody Bellinger leave in free agency, while signing just four significant free agents—J.D. Martinez, Noah Syndergaard, David Peralta, and Shelby Miller—all to one-year deals. The moves were aimed at getting the payroll under the Competitive Balance Tax threshold for 2023. But MLB threw a wrench into that with their ruling on the contract status of Dodgers pitcher Trevor Bauer, who was serving a suspension. The Dodgers would go over the CBT despite their frugal winter.

"I would have to go back and look at it," Friedman said in 2024. "But my guess is we offered some [multi-year contracts] and just didn't line up. It wasn't like a clear, 'We are not going to make any multi-year offers.'"

Nonetheless, some observers believed the Dodgers were willing to accept a "down" season to prepare for their pursuit of Shohei Ohtani when he reached free agency. The Dodgers would "never" have that mindset, Friedman said.

"This is all way too difficult to ever put too much on that and have entire plans around it," Friedman said in 2024. "Because in 2020, that year was really important. In 2021, that year was really important. In 2022, that year was really important. So it's too difficult to say we're going to do everything we can for something that we didn't know how likely it is or not. But it was definitely in the back of our minds, and more than that it got to not doing anything that would tie up the DH position going into this year. That was conscious."

The lack of a DH would not handicap the Dodgers the way it had in 2017. So an aging Justin Turner was not signed after the 2022 season and J.D. Martinez was allowed to leave as a free agent despite an All-Star season as their DH in 2023.

Just days after the Texas Rangers were crowned World Series champions, baseball's off-season officially began as the 30 GMs convened for their annual meetings in Scottsdale, Arizona.

Ohtani's free agency was clearly the top story in the baseball world. But the GMs did their best to say nothing about it.

"He's a special player," Rangers executive vice president and GM Chris Young said.

"He's just such a unique talent," Cleveland Guardians GM Mike Chernoff said.

"He's as fascinating a talent as we've all seen in our generation," Rays president of baseball operations Erik Neander said.

"He's a very good baseball player," Dodgers GM Brandon Gomes ventured with a smile.

"There are 30 teams that would love to have him," Mariners president of baseball operations Jerry Dipoto said.

Clearly, though, not all 30 teams had the resources to sign Ohtani. Early speculation had Ohtani's contract exceeding the 12-year, $426.5 million extension signed by his former teammate Mike Trout in March 2019.

Only a handful of teams could swim in those deep waters, and the Dodgers were viewed as the clear frontrunners. DraftKings Sportsbook had the Dodgers as -110 favorites to sign Ohtani, with the Giants a distant second, at +550.

It was all pure speculation, though, as Ohtani's agent, Nez Balelo, kept a tight lid on any information about his client's decision-making process—just as he had in 2017.

Balelo acknowledged a preference for secrecy when he told The Athletic in 2020 that "It was important to both of us that we controlled the process, message, and ultimately the announcement" of Ohtani's decision in 2017. Meetings with teams were clandestine affairs, with executives escorted in secrecy to make their presentations to Ohtani.

"It was clearly different," Dodgers team president Stan Kasten said of the "Ohtani Sweepstakes" that would be the central story of the off-season. "What was unusual was how much control they decided they needed to exercise to protect Shohei. I understood that there was the threshold issues of who even gets in to be interviewed. Consequently, all the teams made a showing that was greater than you would ordinarily have. It was not just the GM and the president [of baseball operations]. It was also the manager, it was also the owner, it was also the marketing people. It was the full boat to really assess what the next decade would look like.

"And they did spell out early on that they felt 10 years was about right—not 15 that some people shoot for, not five or six. Ten was the sweet spot, which was fine for us.

"So all of those things were different. I will also tell you in these, the player is not always involved in a lot of these [high-level free agent negotiations]. This one—Shohei was involved every step of the way. And it was our third shot for Shohei."

There was one group that Ohtani and Balelo did not want involved—the media. So much so that ESPN's Jeff Passan reported that Balelo had told interested teams it would be held against them if any news leaked about meetings with Ohtani. Balelo later denied those reports.

"It wasn't that explicit," Friedman said later of any prohibition against discussing negotiations. "But we just knew from Nez that it was important in the process and just in general it was something he wanted teams to avoid. It didn't go as far as, 'If you violate, then this,' which tracked with what we understood about the public persona from afar. So it made sense to us hearing that."

But that threat was still lingering in the air as Ohtani's free agency progressed into December and the baseball world convened in Nashville for the annual Winter Meetings.

And then Dave Roberts broke the silence.

For two days during every Winter Meetings, each major-league manager takes a turn meeting with the media and answering questions about his team's plans and prospects for the next season. When Roberts sat down behind the microphone for his media availability, the questions naturally focused on the state of the Ohtani Sweepstakes. Roberts didn't hesitate when asked if the Dodgers were pursuing Ohtani.

"Yeah, we met with him," Roberts said, sending a ripple of excitement through the assembled reporters who had become accustomed to non-answers on the topic of Ohtani's free agency.

"I would like to be honest, and so we met with Shohei and we talked and I think it went well. I think it went well. But at the end of the day, he's his own man and he's going to do what's best for himself, where he feels most comfortable.

"Clearly, Shohei is our top priority."

Kasten had left Nashville early and was in Utica, New York, preparing to launch the inaugural season of the Professional Women's Hockey League, for which he is a member of the advisory board. All six teams are owned by Guggenheim CEO Mike Walter and his wife, Kimbra.

"He did what? He said what?" Kasten said, re-creating his high-volume reaction when he heard Roberts had discussed the Dodgers' meeting with Ohtani with reporters.

The Dodgers had indeed met with Ohtani days earlier. Stadium tours were postponed and then canceled, and the team store at Dodger Stadium was closed so Ohtani wouldn't be spotted by any fans.

The meeting with the Dodgers lasted three hours and was a more low-key pitch than the one the Dodgers had given in 2017. With six years of experience right down the road in Anaheim, the Dodgers felt safe in assuming that Ohtani would be making his decision with a much different base of information. He already knew Southern California and the Dodgers fairly well, they figured. None of their current players were enlisted as salesmen this time around.

"I think that he had questions for us, just trying to get more of the landscape," Roberts said at the Winter Meetings. "But being in this league for six years, he's got a pretty good idea of the Dodgers, what we're about, the city itself.

"In 2017, I think it was more of an overview and…more of a sell of things that he didn't really know about—the country, the city, the organization, potential role. I think that in this situation, not trying to speak for him, but it's a little bit more narrowed on what his desires are as far as teams. I don't think the sell needed to be as large. I think it was more just kind of feeling, trying to feel what everyday life would look like."

Roberts later said his honesty came out of a mistaken belief that Ohtani's meeting with the Dodgers had already been reported. It had not, and both president of baseball operations Andrew Friedman and GM Brandon Gomes (on site at the Winter Meetings) were shocked by Roberts' public comments.

"I was very taken aback. Really confused," Friedman said months later, measuring his words carefully. "I was in a meeting with all the GMs and the commissioner talking about the draft and different rules changes. I left that and...Doc [Dave Roberts] was still doing interviews and stuff.

"I connected with Nez and got a sense of the situation, got the feeling that it wasn't going to be, in and of itself, a disqualifying point. Then later I was able to catch up with Doc in person."

Reflecting on it in 2024, Roberts admitted that for a while after his interview he thought he might have ruined the Dodgers' chances to sign Ohtani.

"Yes, I did," he said. "I knew what I knew. I thought it was a very sensitive situation. After the fact, when I talked to Shohei and Nez, they said that wasn't even the truth [reports that public comments could disqualify a team].

"So based on what I knew up to that point—I thought I had messed it up."

When Friedman reached Roberts after the interview, "he was upset," Roberts recalled. But the two put it to rest with what Friedman described as "a really good conversation," one lubricated by plenty of whiskey at Brad Paisley's 100-acre ranch nearby. The country singer is a big Dodgers fan and hosted a contingent of Dodgers staffers. The get-together featured selections from Paisley's extensive collection of whiskey and lasted into the early morning hours.

The after-hours gathering eventually included members of the Rays staff, including president of baseball operations Erik Neander. While diminishing Paisley's bourbon supply, Friedman and Neander moved forward in trade talks that would eventually lead to the Dodgers acquiring right-hander Tyler Glasnow from the Rays.

Ohtani also made in-person visits to Oracle Park in San Francisco, where newly hired manager Bob Melvin and former catcher Buster Posey were part of the pitch. He also met with team officials at the Toronto Blue Jays' training complex in Florida.

The Dodgers' front office personnel was still sobering up from the visit to Brad Paisley's ranch when things began heating up in the negotiations with Ohtani. Reports had mused on a contract worth $400 million, maybe even approaching $500 million. But Balelo had a different number in mind—$700 million. It would be the most lucrative contract in the history of professional sports.

"I'd love to have seen my poker face," Friedman said of his reaction when Balelo set the price. "And then as he got more and more into the details, by the end, I was, 'Okay, deal.'"

The key point was Ohtani's offer to defer almost all of the contract—$680 million—taking only a $2 million annual salary for the 10-year length of the deal. The massive deferral would minimize the contract's impact on the annual payroll of Ohtani's new team, allowing them to continue adding players.

"Obviously you hear that number [$700 million] and, yeah, that's a big number," Gomes said. "But understanding how it was structured and the reason behind it, it was, wow, that's actually really impressive to have that thought of, 'This is about everybody accomplishing their goals in this.'"

Balelo called it "a unique, historic contract for a unique, historic player." The idea to defer such a large amount was

Ohtani's, his agent said later, a reflection of his true priority—to be part of a championship-caliber team.

"There's no need to defend yourself on this because it is the most incredible act of unselfishness and willingness to win that I've ever experienced in my life or ever will. He did not care at all about the present value inflation. And you know what? Neither did I," Balelo told USA Today Sports.

"He should be praised for this. He did not want to handcuff a team with his salary."

Still—$700 million is a shocking number.

"I think Thursday night was when we were given the numbers," Kasten recalled later. "It started with, I'm on the phone. He [Andrew Friedman] calls me and the first thing he says is, 'Holy fuck.' And I said, 'Is that "Holy fuck" good or "Holy fuck" bad?' He said, 'Holy fuck really good.'

"So he starts with the really big numbers, so it's not really good yet. But then he gives me the [deferrals]. I just said, 'Andrew, we can make that work.' [And Friedman said] 'Yeah, we can.'"

Friedman called the deferral aspect of the contract negotiations "shocking." The Dodgers have frequently negotiated deferrals into contracts with players. Both Mookie Betts ($115 million) and Freddie Freeman ($57 million) deferred large portions of their contracts with the Dodgers. When outfielder Teoscar Hernández signed as a free agent weeks after Ohtani, he agreed to defer $8.5 million of his one-year, $23.5 million contract. When catcher Will Smith signed a 10-year, $140 million extension in March 2024, he agreed to defer $5 million annually.

But Friedman scoffed at the idea that the Dodgers would suggest Ohtani defer 97 percent of his contract.

"The people who think it was our brainchild are definitely overstating our guts," he said. "By the end of him [Balelo] walking through everything—'Okay, deal.' He said, 'I need to bring this to all the interested teams' or all the teams Shohei would potentially be willing to go to and see how many say, "Yes," and then Shohei is going to sleep on it and make a decision.'

"That was the Thursday night before his decision."

At that point, all indications are the field had been narrowed to four teams—the Dodgers, Blue Jays, Giants, and Angels.

Giving the Angels an opportunity to match the $700 million contract offer on the table was more of a courtesy on Ohtani's part. The Angels never showed any willingness to extend themselves that far financially to keep him, something Ohtani essentially admitted in September 2024.

"I think other teams, including the Dodgers, evaluated me highly," Ohtani said. "Rather than think about what the Angels did or didn't do, I'm grateful for the teams that evaluated me highly."

When asked if he would have returned to the Angels if they agreed to the $700 million contract, Ohtani said it was a moot point.

"In reality, I wasn't made an offer, so I can't say," he said. "In reality, I'm doing my best with this team and I'm doing my best with the goal of winning the World Series. I think I'm fine with that."

The Giants were much more serious suitors. President of baseball operations (and former Dodgers GM) Farhan Zaidi later detailed the Giants' efforts to sign Ohtani.

"The proposal that was made was very comparable if not identical to what he wound up agreeing to," Zaidi told reporters on a conference call days after Ohtani signed with the Dodgers. "We offered what would have been the biggest contract in major-league history. I'm guessing we weren't the only team that did that. But we wanted to show our aggressiveness and interest right out of the gate.

"We said we were agreeable to it. It was going to come down to a choice by the player at that point."

The Giants' offer was the same as the Dodgers' offer in "structure and total compensation," Zaidi said. But Zaidi emerged from the meetings with Ohtani—restricted to Oracle Park so that the two-time MVP wouldn't be spotted in San Francisco—with a feeling that the Giants were "disadvantaged just in terms of player preference—geography, in particular."

Geography made the Blue Jays the dark horse among the finalists for Ohtani. But the high-stakes free agency took another odd turn right at the end.

The morning after Friedman said Belelo told him he would be taking the final offer to teams, Friedman said they spoke again.

"I had a really good call with Nez that Friday morning, talking through details, giving him feedback on what he had laid out the night before," Friedman said. "Then a report comes out about him [Ohtani] and the Blue Jays and I'm, 'Eh, that doesn't really make sense.' More and more come out that make it seem more credible. In one of the articles, there was a mention of one of the guys at Rogers [Communications, owners of the Blue Jays], who is a very obscure person when it comes to baseball reporting, that I felt added more credibility to it.

"So then I'm like, 'Okay, I've got to call Nez.' So I call and he red-phones me [declines the call]. So then I'm like, 'Oh my God, this is real.' So for that eight to 10 minutes as I'm updating Mark [Walter, the Dodgers' controlling owner] and Stan [Kasten, team president and CEO], I'm more and more convinced that this is real."

The excitement started with a tweet from MLB Network reporter Jon Morosi, saying Ohtani's decision was "imminent." That was the last thing reported accurately that day.

A fan site, Dodgers Nation, was the first to jump out on the limb when J.P. Hoornstra posted that Ohtani had chosen the Blue Jays. He cited "multiple sources," who were left unnamed.

Even as multiple reporters shot down that Ohtani had chosen the Blue Jays, a story spread that Blue Jays pitcher Yusei Kikuchi had reserved an entire sushi restaurant in downtown Toronto for that night—perhaps for a big celebration with his countryman?

Morosi took it a step further, reporting that Ohtani was physically en route to Toronto. Flight-tracker websites like FlightAware were flooded with fans following a private jet that had left John Wayne Airport in Santa Ana, California, with a flight plan for Toronto. Was Ohtani on his way north?

"It was a bad day," Kasten said, while comparing it to following election results. "All day we're watching that. We're reading Twitter. Toronto never made sense to me—and what must the Toronto [Blue Jays] people have been thinking? They know he's not coming, right? But we weren't talking to them. So we didn't know what was going on. That was an agonizing day."

Dodgers GM Brandon Gomes echoed that, saying "it felt like one of the longest days of my life."

"We were all riding the wave like everybody else and you would feel like we have more information. We just didn't," Gomes said. "Reaching out to Nez, he was, 'Okay, it's not true.' You play that back in your mind and it's, 'Of course, he has to say that.' It's a lose-lose. He has to say that no matter what, because Shohei wants to announce it himself. It was a long, long day. A real rollercoaster. I was going to a dinner with my wife and kids and some neighbors down the street and I'm thinking, 'I am going to be so useless. So not into this.'"

Kasten has butted heads with agents in multiple sports over multiple decades. He is no fan of their ilk. But he gives Balelo credit.

"Nez was truthful with us that entire day," Kasten said later. "That threw us off. We weren't necessarily believing it, even though in retrospect we know he had been telling us the truth.

"I have to say in every step over the month it took [to sign Ohtani]—he never had a reason to lie. He didn't have to find a 'mystery team.' He didn't need to do it."

Friedman said Balelo eventually called him back that Friday night.

"He was, 'Hey, what's up?'" Friedman recalled. "'What do you mean, "what's up?" These public reports.' He's, 'Yeah, they're not true.' 'But, Nez, I know that it was important to Shohei to release this on Instagram. Therefore, you can't tell me it's true.' And he's like, 'You're right. But it's not true.' 'I get it. But again, you can't tell me differently.' So he's like, 'All I can tell you is Shohei is working out right now in Southern California. He is not on a plane to Toronto.… You're just going to have to trust me.'

"'Okay, fair enough. I appreciate it. Thanks.' So at this point I'm off the ledge. But I'm not sure what to make of it, because I feel like with Shohei's desire to announce this on Instagram that Nez had no choice but to tell me that, even if it were true."

But the best story of the day belonged to Dodgers manager Dave Roberts. He was golfing when the false reports began circulating. But he wasn't alone—he was golfing with actor Brian Baumgartner, best known as Kevin, the likeable but dull-witted accountant on the American version of the popular sitcom *The Office*. Roberts had met the actor—and baseball fan—at some point and both were avid golfers. So they planned to play a round together.

"I was at Rancho Santa Fe Country Club, playing the worst round of my life," Roberts recounted months later. "I'm hitting balls over there. Or I would hit on a par-3 and skull the ball that far [pointing 30 yards away]. I was so bad. On the 13th hole, I just said [to Baumgartner], 'I'm sorry. I promise I'm not this bad.' I was a burden. I felt so bad. But he took it like a champ."

The strange day added another Hollywood twist when that private plane from John Wayne Airport landed at Toronto's Pearson International Airport. On board was not Shohei Ohtani but Canadian businessman Robert Herjavec, one of the hosts on the television show *Shark Tank*, along with his family.

"I'm not @shoheiohtani and he was not on my plane today!" Herjavec posted on Instagram. "Not sure how it all started but I'm calling the jays and seeing if they'll sign my 5 year old for 600 mil (he WAS on the plane and throws a mean pitch)"

Shortly after Herjavec's plane landed, Morosi posted an apology on Twitter for reporting "inaccurate information."

Hoornstra, meanwhile, doubled down, defending his reporting in a second post Saturday morning and claiming the Dodgers had increased their offer at the last minute. That was not true either.

A week later, Balelo told USA Today Sports that he met with Ohtani that night to discuss his final decision and their plan to announce it on Ohtani's Instagram account.

"That was about the most reckless reporting I've ever experienced in this game," Balelo told reporter Bob Nightengale.

Ohtani might have been the only character in the drama of his free agency who slept peacefully that night, having told Balelo he wanted to sign with the Dodgers.

"The next day I think there's a decent chance it's going to happen but I'm not even positive his decision is going to be that day," Andrew Friedman said. "So I drop my son off at his soccer game at 11. He's got warmup from 11 to 12. I've scheduled a Zoom call with a player and agent, so I'm sitting in my car with my laptop on a Zoom call and looking to tie this up at 11:55 to get there for the kickoff at noon.

"At about 11:53, 11:54, somewhere around there—the call is starting to wind down but it's not finished yet and I see on my cell a call from Nez. So I'm, 'Hey, guys, I've got to jump. Really appreciate it. Thanks.'"

Friedman got out of his car and answered Balelo's call as he walked toward the field where his son's soccer game was about to start.

"He was like, 'Are you sitting down?'" Friedman said. "'No, I'm actually walking,' and he said, 'You've got him.' 'Excuse me?' 'Shohei's a Dodger.'"

And Friedman's reaction?

"'Holy shit,'" he said. "He was, 'Keep this really tight right now. In the next five minutes, he's going to put it out on Instagram.' So I reached out to Stan [Kasten] and Mark [Walter] and Gomer [Brandon Gomes]. Then on our Slack thread at 11:59 I put out that Shohei is a Dodger and my phone started smoking."

Ohtani's Instagram post ending the most anticipated and scrutinized free agency in baseball history read:

> To all the fans and everyone involved in the baseball world, I apologize for taking so long to come to a decision. I have decided to choose the Dodgers as my next team.
>
> First of all, I would like to express my sincere gratitude to everyone involved with the Angels organization and the fans who have supported me over the past six years, as well as to everyone involved with each team that was part of this negotiation process. Especially to the Angels fans who supported me through all the ups and downs, your guys' support and cheer meant the world to me. The six years I spent with the Angels will remain etched in my heart forever.
>
> And to all Dodger fans, I pledge to always do what's best for the team and always continue to give it my all to be the best version of myself. Until the last day of my playing career, I want to continue to strive forward not only for the Dodgers but for the baseball world.
>
> There are some things that cannot be conveyed in writing so I would like to talk more about this again at a later press conference.
>
> Thank you very much.

Hideki Okuda of *Sports Nippon* said Ohtani's fans were not surprised by their favorite player's choice—finally—of the Dodgers.

"They expected it," Okuda said during the 2024 season. "Some people said [he would go back to the] Anaheim Angels. But maybe 60 percent, 70 percent of the people expected Shohei Ohtani's next team to be the Los Angeles Dodgers.

"So—not surprised. We expected him to be a Dodger—maybe the Toronto Blue Jays. But, no."

The press conference came five days later and filled the center-field plaza at Dodger Stadium. It was televised internationally. Approximately 300 reporters, photographers, and camera operators were credentialed and attended the press conference. MLB Network estimated the viewing audience was 70 million.

"I was told it was only media today," Ohtani said. "So I was not expecting this many people."

Dodgers broadcaster Joe Davis, hosting the press conference, told Ohtani that the large crowd was indeed just media (with a number of team staff mixed in).

Ohtani acknowledged that there were numerous factors that led to his decision to sign with the Dodgers. But the chance to play for championships was "on the top of my list," he said. When team officials like Mark Walter and Andrew Friedman talked to him, Ohtani said, they made it clear they felt winning just one World Series while making the playoffs 11 years in a row was a disappointment and a failure.

"When I heard that, I knew they were all about winning," Ohtani said through his interpreter at the time, Ippei Mizuhara. "I can't wait to join the Dodgers. They share the same passion as me. They have vision and history all about winning and I share the same values. I just can't wait to join the team and get it going."

In addition to the unprecedented deferrals, it was also revealed that Ohtani's contract included a "Key Man" clause—if either Walter or Friedman are no longer with the Dodgers, Ohtani can opt out of his contract.

"Everybody has to be on the same page to be a winning organization," Ohtani said. "I feel almost like I'm having a contract with those two guys."

Ohtani was unequivocal about his goals for their 10-year partnership in Los Angeles.

"I want to win championships," he said. "When people look back at the championships, I want people to feel like I was at the core of those championships."

Friedman wasted little time using the flexibility Ohtani's unique contract gave him to add more pieces he hoped would make the Dodgers champions.

Within a few weeks of Ohtani's signing, the Dodgers landed Japanese right-hander Yoshinobu Yamamoto, giving him a 12-year, $325 million deal—the largest contract ever signed by a pitcher who had yet to throw a pitch in MLB. They traded for Rays right-hander Tyler Glasnow and signed him to a five-year, $136.5 million contract extension. Ohtani took part in the recruiting of each.

"It essentially was, 'I hope you sign with the Dodgers and I want to hit a lot of home runs for you and the team' and stuff like that," Glasnow said of the video he received from the Dodgers featuring Ohtani.

The spending continued in January with the additions of free agent outfielder Teoscar Hernández and pitcher James Paxton. The Dodgers' holiday shopping had them committing $1.2 billion (including the posting fee for Yamamoto) to new additions.

Would the Dodgers have made those other moves without Ohtani's willingness to defer so much of his salary?

"The deal is valued at $46 million a year [in present-day salary], then I would say [it had] no impact," Friedman said. "But if we had done $70 million [a year]—which I don't believe we would have done without deferrals—it does a lot. So it's what you're anchoring it to, which is lost a lot in that question.

"I think people are, 'Oh, on the other side of this is just $70 million with no deferrals. Then could you have done these other things?' Well, I don't think we would have done that.

"But I would say, adding Shohei made us more aggressive because of how good we felt we were and the benefits at that point of where our roster was."

The Dodgers weren't the only ones to benefit from Ohtani's signing—so did pitcher Joe Kelly's wife, Ashley.

During his free agency, Ashley Kelly had publicly campaigned for Ohtani to sign with the Dodgers. In videos posted to her social media accounts, she offered up her husband's uniform number, 17. In what she called her "Ohtake17" campaign, Kelly posted humorous videos showing all of the No. 17 Dodgers gear she had collected over the years and offered to change it from "Kelly" to "Ohtani" and even personalize it for members of his family.

After Ohtani agreed to his contract with the Dodgers, Ashley posted a video of her dancing on her front lawn, spreading No. 17 Dodgers gear among the Christmas decorations—even changing the name of their youngest child, Kai, to "ShoKai" on his Christmas stocking. At the end of the video, she revealed Joe Kelly's new uniform number, 99.

On Christmas Eve, she was rewarded for brokering the number swap when a new silver Porsche pulled up in front of the Kelly residence.

"It's yours. From Shohei," the delivery driver told her on a video posted to the Dodgers' social media accounts. "He wanted to gift you a Porsche."

"Shut the..." Ashley Kelly is heard responding before covering her mouth in surprise.

The car was a four-door Taycan with a sticker price over $100,000—but Ohtani probably didn't pay that. He is a brand ambassador for Porsche and has appeared in ads for the luxury vehicle company.

Joe Kelly said he never discussed any deal with Ohtani and only joked about what he would demand in return for his jersey number.

"I wasn't going to give it up to just anybody," Kelly said. "If Shohei keeps performing, he'll be a future Hall of Famer and I'll be able to have my number retired. That's the closest I'll get to the Hall of Fame."

Chapter 2

Spring of Changes

So much changed for the Los Angeles Dodgers after they signed Shohei Ohtani. But nothing really changed.

The Dodgers' billion-dollar splurge to add Ohtani, Yoshinobu Yamamoto, Tyler Glasnow, Teoscar Hernández, and James Paxton to a team that won over 100 games in each of the previous four full seasons—a streak no other MLB team had ever matched—marked them as a favorite to win the World Series in 2024. But the Dodgers had frequently been World Series contenders, if not favorites, over the past decade.

The team made the playoffs in each of the 11 seasons before 2024, dominating the National League West to win the division title in 10 of those seasons. They had five 100-win seasons since 2017 and averaged 99 wins in the past 10 full seasons. Three times they advanced to the World Series—2017, 2018, and 2020.

But all that winning produced just one championship—following the pandemic-shortened 2020 season. Every other season has been a failure. That is the standard the Dodgers have created.

"We've got one goal every year and that's to win the World Series, and that's just who we are," Freddie Freeman acknowledged.

A member of the teams that reached the World Series in 2017, 2018, and 2020, Kiké Hernández left as a free agent only to return in a trade during the 2023 season. He found the same "World Series or Bust" expectations.

"I mean, it's fair," the utilityman said of those annual expectations. "We don't play here to make the playoffs. We play here to win the World Series, and if we don't win it, it's a failure. How many years has this team made the playoffs in a row? Division championships only get you so far. They're not building this team to make it to October. They're building it to go deep in October and win a World Series."

In recent years, the Dodgers have come up far short of that lofty goal. They were eliminated in their first postseason series three times between 2019 and 2023.

In 2019, it was the eventual World Series champions, the Washington Nationals, who stunned the Dodgers in the final game of their best-of-five National League Division Series. Dodgers starter Walker Buehler pitched brilliantly and handed a 3–1 lead over to the bullpen in the seventh inning. But the Dodgers turned to their ace, Clayton Kershaw, to pitch in relief, and he gave up back-to-back home runs to Anthony Rendon and Juan Soto in the eighth. Veteran reliever Joe Kelly gave up the series-deciding grand slam to Howie Kendrick in the 10th inning.

After winning their "bubble" championship in 2020, the Dodgers reached the National League Championship Series in 2021 only to lose to the Atlanta Braves.

In 2022, the Dodgers won 111 games during the regular season and matched up in the NLDS with a San Diego Padres team they had thoroughly dominated. The Dodgers had won 23 of the previous 28 meetings with the Padres and outscored them 109–47 during that year's 19 matchups. It looked like more of the same when the Dodgers took Game 1 of the series.

But the Padres eliminated them in four games. The Dodgers blew a 3–0 lead in the seventh inning of the decisive Game 4.

The 22-win difference in their regular-season records was the largest in a postseason upset since the 93-win Chicago White Sox defeated the 116-win Chicago Cubs in the 1906 World Series.

"Shock factor—very high. Disappointment—very high. It's crushing," Roberts said in the immediate aftermath.

But there was another lightning strike waiting for the Dodgers in October 2023.

Their NLDS matchup with the Arizona Diamondbacks seemed as lopsided on paper as the 2022 matchup with the Padres. The Diamondbacks had finished a distant second to the Dodgers in the NL West, with 16 fewer wins.

But the Dodgers' starting pitching had dissolved over the course of the season due to injuries and off-field issues. The three starters they sent to the mound against the Diamondbacks— Kershaw, rookie Bobby Miller, and midseason trade acquisition Lance Lynn—combined to record a total of just 14 outs while allowing 13 runs. According to Elias Sports, the 4⅔ innings from the trio were the fewest by the starting pitchers in the first three games of a postseason series in MLB history.

That wasn't the only problem, though. Mookie Betts and Freddie Freeman finished second and third in the NL Most Valuable Player Award voting for their outstanding regular seasons. But they went a combined 1-for-21 in the three-game sweep by the Diamondbacks, the lone hit an infield single by Freeman in the first inning of Game 2.

In the wake of a second consecutive first-round defeat, Dodgers president of baseball operations Andrew Friedman called it "an organizational failure."

"Our goal was to win 11 games in October and we didn't win one," Friedman said. "So we need to figure out what we can do differently and how to go about it."

The Dodgers would deny that their billion-dollar binge during the off-season was strictly motivated by those shocking playoff failures. But the lure of another division title and 100-win regular season would have been diminished and a tough sell to the 3 million fans who annually show up at Dodger Stadium, accustomed—some would say, spoiled—as they have become with that.

Ohtani certainly knew what it would take to satisfy those fans—and justify those investments.

"I mean, the only choice is winning the World Series," he said through his interpreter early in spring.

If the true payoff was months away, all those off-season moves changed the narrative and emotional tone of spring training.

Without the big acquisitions of the winter, the spring would have featured a series of questions from the media, continually probing what had gone wrong the previous Octobers and questioning the direction of a franchise with a trail of unrealized aspirations.

"There's no way around it—we sucked," Max Muncy said during the spring, in looking back at the 2023 NLDS. "We really kind of blew it. And I'm not trying to take anything away from the Diamondbacks. They obviously played very well and hats off to them. But we blew it.

"I feel like you can have a dartboard and throw a dart and it would land on something that went wrong. We didn't do a whole lot right. We didn't hit. We didn't score. We didn't pitch. There really wasn't a whole lot that we did well."

All of that was forgotten—if not forgiven—in the excitement surrounding the arrival of Ohtani and the other newcomers.

Instead, the central question of spring training and the overriding narrative was focused on just how good the 2024 Dodgers could be with a lineup topped by three former MVP winners (Betts, Ohtani, and Freeman) and a rotation fortified by the additions of Glasnow and Yamamoto.

Early in spring camp, Roberts acknowledged the value of personnel changes washing away the recent past.

"I think reshuffling the deck with new players, I think that brought a lot of excitement to the fan base, to the organization itself," he said. "The newness part of it, yeah."

No one brought more of that excitement than Ohtani.

No. 17 Dodgers jerseys flew off the shelves from the moment Ohtani made his announcement on Instagram and could be seen all over the grounds at Camelback Ranch during spring workouts. Advance ticket prices for key games skyrocketed.

"I've never seen anything like it," said 10-year veteran starter James Paxton of the added buzz in spring training centered around Ohtani and Yamamoto. "I've never seen so many fans in spring training. You're out on the back fields. You hear a big cheer go up and you know it's for Ohtani or Yamamoto."

For Ohtani, spring training would be spent adapting to the changes in his life—on the field and off.

After six seasons with the Angels, Ohtani was surrounded by a whole new set of teammates, coaches, and staff members as he reported to spring training. It was like starting all over again, Ohtani admitted.

"I'm on a brand-new team so I'm going to act like I'm a rookie and try to get along with all the guys, get along with my teammates," he said.

"So far all the guys I've met, they've been great. They've been very welcoming so [there are] no issues there."

After signing with the Dodgers in early December, Ohtani worked out at Dodger Stadium for weeks before heading to Arizona. That gave him a chance to meet a number of his new teammates like Gavin Lux and Walker Buehler, who also worked out in Southern California before heading to spring training.

"They keep a lot of data and kind of track everything pretty intently," Buehler said of watching Ohtani work with the Dodgers' player performance staff. "Kind of everything you can do, you see there's a different level of athlete. He's special in that way. It's cool. What's the phrase everyone says? Hard work beats talent when talent doesn't work hard. He kind of does both. It's fun to watch and been cool to see, especially when he's on our side."

Ohtani said he didn't hesitate to initiate those first conversations with his new co-workers.

"I like to go up and say, 'Hi' and introduce myself," he said, adding some dry humor. "But there are so many new people that I have to make sure I don't introduce myself twice. If I do, hopefully they'll let it go."

The signing of Yoshinobu Yamamoto gave Ohtani a fellow countryman as a teammate, and the two Japanese stars had lockers next to each other all spring and again in the home clubhouse at Dodger Stadium. But Ohtani made other friends quickly—most prominently, outfielder Teoscar Hernández.

Hernández and Ohtani met at the 2021 All-Star Game, when both were selected to the American League team, and a friendship was sparked. Why the two with such different backgrounds clicked so quickly, Hernández couldn't explain.

"I don't know. It's one of those relationships when you see a guy you just became in a good spot and start talking to them," Hernández said. "That's what happened. We played against each other. We created that relationship with us. Now that we're together [on the same team], it's even better. I try to enjoy every moment that I talk to him, be around him, and try to learn from him, too—not only about baseball but about his family, too, their culture and everything."

When Hernández signed a one-year deal with the Dodgers in January 2024, Ohtani sent him a message via Instagram—in English—expressing his excitement that they would now be teammates. And Ohtani reached out personally via text.

"He was the first one," Hernández said. "He already signed his contract. It was two, three weeks later that I signed. He was the first one to text me, then Miggy [Rojas] did."

A native of Northern California, second-year outfielder James Outman had a good childhood friend who was Japanese. His friend's family spoke Japanese, and Outman said he remembered a few words and phrases and used them with Ohtani—to the amusement of his new teammate.

Ohtani went out of his way to blend in with his teammates. He and Yamamoto were among the players who attended—but didn't participate in—the team's annual wing-eating contest at a restaurant near its Glendale complex. They even contributed to the prize won by Yamamoto's interpreter, Hiro Sonoda, who ate 69 chicken wings—well beyond the 40 wings that Ohtani estimated he could eat himself.

When video of Ohtani at the event appeared on social media, it was a shock to people with the Angels who had not seen such interaction during his years with them.

Later in spring training, Dodgers manager Dave Roberts invited magician Shlomo Levinger to put on a show for the team during the morning meeting before one day's workout. Levinger performed one trick with Ohtani, placing a boxed deck of cards in Ohtani's hand and telling him to name a card in the deck.

Ohtani chose the seven of diamonds. Levinger tore the box open and pulled out four cards. Written on the backs were the words, *The*, *Seven*, *Of*, and *Diamonds*—to the amazement of Ohtani.

"I think he's fitting in seamlessly so far, which has been awesome to see," Dodgers GM Brandon Gomes said. "Joking around, coming in and really embracing the culture. And on-the-field-wise, his swing looks great. He's progressing really well.

"So it feels like he's in a really good place overall and I think it's been a great transition. He's fitting into the culture exactly as we would have hoped."

Roberts said his early impressions of Ohtani were that he's "a really methodical, really focused worker" but also was "more engaging than I probably would have expected."

That impression, built over Ohtani's years in Anaheim, might have been created by Ohtani's lack of openness with the media and infrequent interviews—something that would change at least a little bit in his first year with the Dodgers.

"Um, maybe. That might be the case, but that's a hard one to answer," Roberts said. "All I know is that with us, as far as when he's working and he's in the clubhouse, talking to his teammates—it's been great. It's been great."

With the Dodgers scheduled to open the season with two games in Korea, on March 20 and 21, spring training began early and had a bit of a compressed schedule. That raised questions about Ohtani's availability to be the Dodgers' DH for the games in Korea, based on his recovery from elbow surgery in September 2023.

The week before spring camp opened, the Dodgers had their DodgerFest fan event at Dodger Stadium. At that point, Ohtani said he was "very confident" he would be in the Dodgers' lineup when they played the San Diego Padres in the Seoul Series.

"We're right on schedule," he said at the February 3 event. "As long as there are no setbacks going forward, I'll be ready."

Early on, the Dodgers eliminated the possibility of Ohtani pitching until 2025. He said the twin tasks of rehabbing long term as a pitcher while rehabbing to play as a hitter in 2024 were manageable.

"This is not my first time doing this, rehabbing while getting ready for the season," Ohtani said, referring to his first Tommy John surgery following the 2018 season. "I did this back in '19, so I kind of know how to do it and I feel like it'll be easier the second time around."

The prospect of Ohtani channeling his resources, energy, and time more exclusively into hitting—for months his only pitching rehab would be light throwing sessions every other day—raised the possibility of him being an even better hitter in 2024.

"I feel like there's not just one level but several levels ahead offense-wise," he said. "It's just going to depend on what kind of lineup I'm in and everything. But at the end, my focus is going to be the same—keep the focus on my hitting and trying to get better."

The first steps in the progression toward being in the Dodgers' lineup involved hitting off a tee during his workouts at Dodger Stadium. Once Ohtani arrived at Camelback Ranch for spring training, those sessions largely happened out of sight.

One of the changes at the Dodgers' spring training complex in 2024 was the presence of "The Lab"—the name given to the 12,000-square-foot building that greeted players upon their arrival. What used to be simply a string of batting cages, open to the elements, just outside the main building was enclosed and expanded to become a two-story facility manned by the organization's player development and performance science groups.

The new setup in 2024 allowed players to take batting practice in a variety of ways—including off a Trajekt Arc virtual reality pitching machine. The Trajekt machine uses high-tech data to mimic the pitches—breaks and velocity—of any big-league pitcher.

The technology in the lab also allows instructors to give players immediate feedback from force plates, motion-capture cameras, and other swing tracking data, and even compare it to data from previous workouts or seasons.

"It's a different sound coming off the bat," Roberts said of watching Ohtani hit in the batting cage. "The barrel accuracy is really good. But the power is really impressive. Just for me to see it up close and personal how much bat speed he generates is very impressive."

Ohtani spent his early spring days working largely in The Lab. When he took his work to one of the practice fields a week into spring training, it was predictably big news, with a large group of reporters gathered outside the practice field and camera operators leaning over the center-field fence to get footage of the event.

It was Ohtani's first time hitting on a baseball field since he injured his oblique on September 4, ending his 2023 season with the Angels early. Two weeks later, he underwent his second reconstructive elbow surgery.

In his first on-field batting practice session with the Dodgers, Ohtani took 21 swings in two rounds of hitting against gameplanning coach J.T. Watkins. Ten of those swings sent a ball soaring over the outfield fence. A tablet tracking Ohtani's results showed exit velocities as high as 109 mph.

"He's explosive, has leverage, speed, strength, the whole thing," Dodgers hitting coach Robert Van Scoyoc said after the exhibition.

Ohtani gave the first batting session a positive review, saying he had planned "to swing on the lighter side" but felt so good that he put more effort into the swings.

"I felt really good overall," he said. "Every swing got really strong with some good results."

The next step in Ohtani's progression would be to face live pitching. It's an annual part of spring training; hitters step in against the team's pitchers as a final preparation before facing opposing teams in exhibition games.

A week after taking his first batting practice on the practice field, Ohtani stepped in for the live batting practice session against veteran relievers Ryan Brasier, Blake Treinen, and J.P. Feyereisen.

Ohtani stood in for five pitches against Brasier without swinging, then faced Treinen for five pitches, fouled one off his foot, and swung-and-missed at the last one.

Ohtani stood in for five more pitches from Feyereisen, turning on the last one and driving Feyereisen's fastball over the center-field fence. Teammate Evan Phillips immediately texted Feyereisen.

"Evan said I should go get the baseball and get it signed by him [Ohtani]," Feyereisen said later.

Ohtani declined to speak to reporters after the workout. So Feyereisen found himself surrounded at his locker, wearing a startled expression when he turned around to find himself facing numerous cameras and a large group of reporters.

"I didn't even know I was facing him, honestly," said Feyereisen, who was making his own return after missing the entire 2023 season due to shoulder surgery. "It was just kind of a live BP and there were, like, 10 hitters in the lineup and these guys you could possibly face.

"When he steps inside the box, he's just another hitter. That's how you're supposed to see it. Obviously with the following that he has, it's a little different. But it's still fun to face him."

Feyereisen joked that everything seemed to go "dead quiet" whenever Ohtani stepped in the batter's box.

"'Shohei is hitting. Let's go watch him,'" Feyereisen imagined everyone saying.

Roberts was certainly happy with what he was seeing in those early weeks of spring training.

"He's a lot further along than I think any of us maybe not named Shohei would have expected," Roberts said. "He's worked really hard, is very diligent in his work. So he's ahead of schedule…. It seems like every single day, he keeps getting better and feels really good."

Ohtani rejected any suggestion that he was ahead of schedule in his rehab. If anything, he was simply meeting his own expectations.

"I don't really feel like it's ahead of schedule. I feel like we're right on schedule, which is a really good thing," he said when told of Roberts' estimate. "And my body is reacting really well so far. So everything is trending in the right direction."

Ohtani estimated that he would need 50 at-bats to get ready for the start of the season. Those at-bats could come in Cactus League games, live batting practice, back-field games on the minor-league side of the training complex, or even just off the Trajekt Arc pitching machine.

"There's not a huge difference within a game or inside," he said. "The main thing I'm looking for is the timing aspect, when I'm late on pitches or early, how my body reacts, how my bat reacts. There's not too big of a difference."

There was a big difference for fans who yearned to see the Dodgers' new $700 million man play in a game for the first time wearing a Dodgers uniform. That came on February 27, when Ohtani made his 2024 Cactus League debut against the Chicago White Sox.

Ohtani got a standing ovation before his first at-bat but struck out against White Sox left-hander Garrett Crochet, taking a 100-mph fastball for a called strike three. In his second at-bat, Ohtani bounced into a double play.

In his third and final at-bat of the day, Ohtani rose to the occasion and gave the fans what they came to see, lofting a high fly ball to left field that carried over the fence for a home run.

"I'm starting to learn really quickly he's built differently," Roberts said of Ohtani rising to the moment—with the help of the dry Arizona air, notorious for enhancing spring home runs.

"I thought I hit it a little too high but maybe the Arizona weather factored in a little," Ohtani himself acknowledged.

Ohtani batted second in his Cactus League debut with the Dodgers, solving one of the mysteries of the spring—how would Roberts arrange his three former MVPs at the top of the lineup? It seemed pretty clear that Mookie Betts would bat leadoff. Freddie Freeman had hit second in 2023, batting .331 with a .976 OPS. But Ohtani had batted second most often during his six years in Anaheim (and had his best offensive numbers when batting there).

"As a manager, you start trying to formulate a lineup and see how it looks on paper," Dave Roberts said during spring training. "You get a big glow on your face when you look at Ohtani, Freeman, and Betts."

The Dodgers manager met privately with each of the three players during the first days of spring camp, letting them know his thoughts on the batting order. What emerged was the order the Dodgers employed to start the season—Betts at leadoff, followed by Ohtani and Freeman.

"There weren't any strong opinions," Roberts said of his conversation with the trio. "I think that having that conversation, but also their openness, was really important. And to a man, they said it doesn't really matter where they hit."

According to Elias Sports Bureau, it was the fifth time in MLB history—and the first time since the 2004 New York Yankees (Alex Rodriguez, Gary Sheffield, and Jorge Posada)—that a team boasted three players who finished in the top three of MVP voting in their leagues the previous season. Ohtani won the American League MVP in 2023; Betts and Freeman finished second and third, respectively, in the NL voting.

When Roberts decided to put them in the first three spots in the batting order—a foregone conclusion from the moment Ohtani signed—it was the first time three former MVPs were batting in the first three spots for a team since the 1983 Philadelphia

Phillies rolled out a lineup with Joe Morgan, Pete Rose, and Mike Schmidt at the top. It has only happened two other times—the 1976 Cincinnati Reds (Rose, Morgan, and Johnny Bench) and the 1978 Reds (Rose, Morgan, and George Foster).

The Phillies went with that order 10 times in 1983, the Reds once each in 1976 and 1978. The Dodgers would roll out their MVPs 1-2-3 nearly every day until Mookie Betts suffered a fractured hand in mid-June.

"I think that if you're looking at the DNA of the two hitters, Shohei is more of a free swinger than Freddie is," Roberts said during spring training while talking through his thought process. "So if you have somebody like Freddie behind him, pitchers are still going to attack Shohei in a specific way, no doubt about it. But there's also a chance that they should be in the strike zone a little bit more than if Freddie wasn't behind him.

"Not to take anything away from anybody else on our roster, but Freddie is the biggest presence for protection behind Shohei."

It took just four Cactus League game appearances for Ohtani to declare his rehab complete, at least as far as his DH duties were concerned.

"I think we can say the hitting part of rehab is officially over," he said after going 0-for-3 on March 5. "Now I just need to get more at-bats, have quality at-bats, be able to see the ball and get my timing down."

Roberts agreed with Ohtani, saying his DH was no longer in "rehab mode" as a hitter with nine games left before the team traveled to South Korea.

"I think right now he's in 'prepare-for-the-season' mode," Roberts said. "Which is a good thing for all of us."

Even bigger news came off the field as February came to an end. Ohtani surprised everyone when he announced on his Instagram account that he was married.

"To all my friends and fans throughout, I have an announcement to make," he posted. "Not only have I began a new chapter in my career with the Dodgers but I also have began a new life with someone from my Native country of Japan who is very special to me and I wanted everyone to know I am now married.

"I am excited for what is to come and thank you for your support."

He gave no more details in the announcement, which caught even the tenacious Japanese media off guard. The news immediately became the top story on Japanese television.

"I'm very happy for him and his bride," Dave Roberts said, adding that the news caught Ohtani's Dodgers teammates by surprise as well. "As far as wedding gifts, we got surprised and didn't have much time to think about it."

Agreeing to speak with the media at Camelback Ranch, Ohtani remained secretive, declining to provide his wife's name.

"She is a Japanese woman," he said through his interpreter. "I don't really feel comfortable talking about when I got married exactly. But she's a normal Japanese woman."

Ohtani said he and his wife had known each other for three or four years and got engaged in 2023. But he would not be specific about when their wedding had been.

"I felt like it was good timing because it was before the season," Ohtani said. "I didn't really want any distractions once the season started. I would have liked to announce it earlier but there were some paperwork issues that [delayed] the whole process."

Identifying his wife as "a normal Japanese woman" only delayed the inevitable. Media went to work trying to learn her identity.

It didn't take long before Mamiko Tanaka was identified as Ohtani's bride.

The 27-year-old Tanaka is a former professional basketball player who played at Waseeda University before joining the Fujitsu Red Wave of the women's professional league in Japan in 2019. A 5-foot-11 forward, Tanaka played in 28 games for Fujitsu in her fourth and final season in 2023.

Her former team released a statement congratulating their onetime forward.

"We wish to celebrate from the bottom of our hearts the new journey embarked by Mamiko Tanaka who provided joy to many people through her performances with the Fujitsu Red Wave," it read. "We pray this new stage of life will be wonderful for the two of them."

The couple's unofficial coming-out occurred when the Dodgers traveled to Korea for their season-opening games against the Padres. The Dodgers' social media team posted a photo of Shohei and Mamiko getting off the plane together in Seoul on the team's Instagram and X accounts, identifying Tanaka as Ohtani's wife in the text. The two were also seen in tandem during video of the team boarding the plane to Korea.

The photos caused a stir on the Internet as Ohtani's fans learned about Tanaka. Later, during the Dodgers' stay in Seoul, the team organized a dinner at their hotel, after which photos of Shohei and Mamiko meeting tennis legend (and owner of a minority stake in the Dodgers) Billie Jean King found their way to social media.

Tanaka earned approval from fans who noted that the small shoulder bag she was holding in the photo was a Zara handbag which sells for about $30, a modest fashion choice for the wife of a multi-millionaire global celebrity.

During broadcasts of the Dodgers' games at Gocheok SkyDome in Seoul, cameras frequently found Tanaka in the stands where she watched with Ohtani's mother and sister—so much so that SportsNet LA's producers were asked to stop behind the scenes (even though they had no control of the international feed being used back in the United States).

Ohtani's marriage was even a topic during a press conference featuring Ohtani, Betts, and Freeman before the Dodgers' first workout in Seoul. One reporter asked Ohtani for details about his marriage—including his courtship of Mamiko.

The question drew laughter from Betts and Freeman, already well versed in Ohtani's preference for privacy from media scrutiny. Freeman reached for the translating device in front of him and quickly slipped in the earpiece.

"I gotta hear this," Freeman said. "Go ahead, Sho. Spill it."

Ohtani wasn't about to share any details. He smiled sheepishly at Freeman's teasing and swatted away the reporter's pitch.

"I answered all of the questions in an interview earlier, so I don't really want to," he said, referring to his brief detail-free interview in Arizona and drawing laughter. "But it is the first time she's coming to a game with me so I think it's going to be really great memories for both of us. But, like I said earlier, I'm focused on baseball."

Ohtani had no idea at the time how that focus would be challenged by more seismic changes in his life.

Chapter 3

"Beyond Shocked"

Baseball and gambling have had a tangled relationship from the earliest days of professional teams in the 1800s. Players were banned for allegedly throwing games as far back as 1865 by the National Association of Baseball Players.

The second World Series in 1905 featured the New York Giants and Philadelphia A's. Hall of Fame manager John McGraw had not let his team play in the 1904 World Series, a consequence of his feud with American League president Ban Johnson.

But in 1905, McGraw not only led his Giants into the World Series but also let it be known publicly that he had wagered $400 on his team to win—a bet he collected with no consequences after his team beat the A's, four games to one.

Some of the biggest scandals in the history of Major League Baseball have involved gambling—most famously the Black Sox scandal of 1919.

Owner Charles Comiskey's Chicago White Sox had already won the World Series in 1917 and featured some of the game's biggest stars in Eddie Collins and "Shoeless Joe" Jackson. But a faction of the team saw Comiskey as a miser who underpaid them, and resented it—though the White Sox's 1919 payroll (such as it was in the days of the reserve clause binding players to one team for life) was the highest in baseball.

Gamblers swarmed around baseball in those days, with rumors—founded and unfounded—of fixes on a regular basis. On the eve of the 1919 World Series, White Sox first baseman Chick Gandil told Joe "Sport" Sullivan, a known bookie from Boston, that he could throw the Series for $80,000.

Details got murky in the aftermath of the scandal. Shoeless Joe was apparently not at the pre-Series meeting arranging the fix. Third baseman Buck Weaver was at the meeting but claimed he didn't take any money from the gamblers.

Regardless, rumors that the fix was in spread so thoroughly that the odds against the underdog Cincinnati Reds shifted greatly. Several reporters covering the World Series—including Hall of Fame player Christy Mathewson—decided to compare notes on questionable plays.

Sox ace Red Faber came down with the flu and was unable to pitch in the Series, giving the plan to throw games a boost. Instead, Eddie Cicotte started Game 1 and hit the first batter he faced—a sign to gamblers that the Sox were about to throw the Series.

The White Sox lost the best-of-nine Series in eight games— but only after winning Games 6 and 7 when the promised payments were slow to come. Threats of violence were made against players and their family members before the decisive Game 8.

Rumors of the World Series fix followed the White Sox into the 1920 season, and eventually a grand jury was formed to investigate. Cicotte and three others confessed to their part in the scheme and Comiskey suspended the seven players involved who were still playing for the Sox.

None of the players were found guilty in court but team owners hired Kenesaw Mountain Landis, a federal judge, to clean up the game and restore confidence in the integrity of Major League Baseball. Landis became the game's first commissioner, and one of his first acts was to place eight members of the Black Sox on a newly created "ineligible list," banning them from organized baseball for life. Two other players—Hal Chase (notorious for his involvement with gamblers) and Joe Gedeon—were also placed on the ineligible list for their tangential link to the scandal.

Shoeless Joe became a mythical character after the Black Sox scandal. It is questionable how much he did to throw the Series. His defenders would point out that Jackson hit .375 in the eight games, the highest of any player, and made no errors in the field. He even drove in six runs in the five games the Sox lost.

For decades, supporters tried to clear the names of Weaver and Jackson, unsuccessfully.

Landis eventually banned 19 people for various offenses, including 12 players for gambling. Scarred by the Black Sox scandal, Major League Baseball stayed vigilant about anything that seemed to hint at the influence of gambling. The last pitcher to win 30 games in a season, Denny McLain, was suspended for three months in 1970 for his involvement in bookmaking operations.

L.A. STORY

That vigilance became overzealous when legendary players Willie Mays and Mickey Mantle were banned from baseball for "associating" with gamblers long after their playing days had ended.

Their association consisted of signing on as "goodwill ambassadors" for a pair of Atlantic City casinos—Mays in 1979, Mantle in 1983. Their jobs involved shaking hands at corporate events or playing golf with patrons.

Atlantic City did not even allow sports betting at the time and, as casino employees, Mays and Mantle were not allowed by law to gamble in any Atlantic City casino. Nonetheless, MLB commissioner Bowie Kuhn barred Mays and Mantle from working with any MLB team. Both had been working only as part-time instructors with the Mets and Yankees, respectively.

"A casino is no place for a baseball hero and Hall of Famer," Kuhn huffed—an ironic stance given the number of casinos and sportsbooks that are now sponsors and corporate partners with MLB.

When Peter Ueberroth succeeded Kuhn as commissioner, one of his first acts was to reinstate Mays and Mantle, in the spring of 1985.

Four years later, a much more serious gambling scandal rocked baseball.

Sports Illustrated was the first to report that Pete Rose, baseball's all-time hits leader as a player and the Reds' manager at the time, had bet on baseball games while playing and/or managing the Reds. Rose's pervasive gambling habit extended far beyond baseball, but the allegations that he bet on Reds games led to an investigation by MLB. Commissioner Bart

54

Giamatti named John Dowd, formerly an attorney for the U.S. Department of Justice, as special counsel.

Rose denied publicly that he had ever bet on baseball—a stance that would fluctuate over the years until he published a book in 2004 and admitted to it. Dowd's report to Giamatti led to a lifetime ban for Rose, who signed an agreement with Giamatti that declared him permanently ineligible without a formal declaration that Rose had indeed bet on baseball.

Rose later went to prison for tax evasion and made a living on his infamy, signing autographs and selling memorabilia. For years, he would set up a table in Cooperstown during induction weeks—part of baseball's annual tableau but not part of the HOF.

He has never appeared on a Hall of Fame ballot. Two commissioners (Fay Vincent and Bud Selig) declined to act on Rose's applications for reinstatement. In 2015, Rob Manfred rejected the request. Rose passed away in 2024.

The current landscape of sports gambling in the United States has changed drastically from the shadowy underworld of illegal bookmakers into which Rose and others sank.

Now, there is a statue of Pete Rose outside the home plate entrance to Cincinnati's Great American Ball Park, home of the Reds. Frozen in his iconic "Charlie Hustle" headfirst dive, the statue's arms point across the street to a BetMGM sports book where fans can place bets on a variety of events before heading into a Reds game.

It is an increasingly common combination.

There are sportsbooks from BetMGM at Nationals Park in Washington, D.C., from Caesars outside Chase Field in Phoenix, and from DraftKings at Wrigley Field. The outfield walls at Citi Field feature ads for Caesars Sportsbook. In Toronto, one of the Blue Jays' sponsors at Rogers Centre is theScore Bet Sportsbook and Casino.

The list goes on.

MLB's relationship with gambling was upended after a Supreme Court ruling in May 2018 allowed states to decide individually if they wanted to legalize sports betting. As of the summer of 2024, 38 of the 50 states have legalized sports gambling in some form.

Sports betting apps have become ubiquitous. Ads promoting BetMGM, FanDuel, Draft Kings, and others have proliferated on sports broadcasts and websites and inside stadiums. Athletes and celebrities appear in commercials promoting sports gambling venues.

To say sports gambling has become a lucrative partner for sports leagues, TV networks, and governments (through tax revenue) is an understatement. Statista.com estimated more than $11 billion was wagered legally in the United States in 2023.

Some of that was wagered by professional athletes. Professional baseball, football, and basketball have disciplined players in recent years for their involvement with legal sports betting.

Tucupita Marcano, a marginal big-leaguer with the San Diego Padres and Pittsburgh Pirates, was banned for life in 2024 for wagering more than $150,000 on 387 baseball bets with a legal sportsbook.

Four other players were suspended for one year for making smaller bets on baseball. MLB's collective bargaining agreement with the players' union allows players to bet on sports other than baseball, as long as it is with a legal sportsbook. Team employees are also subject to the same prohibitions.

It is that distinction that led to baseball's biggest gambling scandal since Pete Rose's banishment.

Born in Japan but raised mostly in Southern California, Ippei Mizuhara moved back to Japan in 2013 when he was hired to serve as an interpreter for former (and future) big-league pitcher Chris Martin and other English-speaking players on the Nippon Ham Fighters in Japan's professional baseball league.

Shohei Ohtani also joined the Fighters as an 18-year-old rookie that year.

When Ohtani moved to the United States to play for the Los Angeles Angels in 2018, Mizuhara went with him and became a constant presence, always at Ohtani's side as he navigated the intense media scrutiny his success as a two-way player created.

"I saw two guys who were the best of friends," former Angels manager Phil Nevin said of the relationship between the two.

Mizuhara's father was a chef in the Anaheim area, and Ohtani and his interpreter would eat at that restaurant almost daily when the Angels were in town. Mizuhara would often catch for Ohtani during off-season workouts and even served as the catcher during Ohtani's participation in the 2021 Home Run Derby at Coors Field in Colorado.

Mizuhara was an all-purpose, right-hand man for Ohtani, essentially acting as his manager while also performing an assortment of duties, like bringing him groceries during the COVID lockdown—and setting up bank accounts.

At some point during Ohtani's years with the Angels, Mizuhara became involved with an illegal bookmaking operation run by alleged bookmaker Mathew Bowyer, in California—one of the 12 remaining states that has not legalized sports gambling.

A former commodities trader (among other abandoned enterprises) who listed $425,000 in losses to two Las Vegas casinos in his 2011 bankruptcy filing, Bowyer became the target of a federal investigation into illegal gambling in Southern California that centered on Wayne Nix, a former minor-league pitcher turned bookie. That investigation also ensnared former Dodger Yasiel Puig and David Fletcher, a former teammate of Ohtani's with the Angels.

Mizuhara said he met Bowyer at a poker game in San Diego in 2021. Mizuhara soon began wagering on international soccer, basketball, and football through Bowyer or his associates—one of whom was later revealed to allegedly be Ryan Boyajian, a cast member of the reality TV series, *The Real Housewives of Orange County*.

Federal investigators found evidence that Mizuhara placed approximately 19,000 bets between December 2021 and January 2024. Mizuhara won more than $142 million—but lost $183 million. He placed an average of 25 bets per day for amounts ranging from $10 to $160,000. There was no evidence he ever placed a bet on Major League Baseball. Bowyer extended credit to Mizuhara, confident he could pay given his proximity to Ohtani.

Mizuhara turned to Ohtani to cover his losses.

Federal investigators found that Mizuhara changed the contact phone number and email attached to a bank account he opened for Ohtani in Arizona to a number and email linked to Mizuhara, not Ohtani. That allowed Mizuhara to prevent the bank from notifying Ohtani about any account activity.

After Mizuhara was charged with bank and tax fraud, prosecutors alleged that Mizuhara got the bank to approve large wire transfers from Ohtani's account, even impersonating Ohtani on phone calls, recordings of which were obtained by authorities.

"The extent of this defendant's deception and theft is massive," U.S. Attorney for the Central District of California Martin Estrada said in a news release. "He took advantage of his position of trust to take advantage of Mr. Ohtani and fuel a dangerous gambling habit."

Mizuhara also allegedly used Ohtani's account to pay for $60,000 worth of dental work and purchase $325,000 worth of collectible baseball cards, hoping to sell them for a profit.

Mizuhara's gambling first hit the news in March 2024, as the Dodgers were about to open the season with two historic games in Seoul, South Korea.

Reporters at ESPN had learned of the federal investigation into Bowyer and that it included wire transfers with Ohtani's name on them. Mizuhara was contacted by ESPN and, during a 90-minute interview on March 19 (arranged by Ohtani's representatives), claimed that Ohtani had agreed to the wire transfers in order to help Mizuhara pay off his gambling debts, logging into Ohtani's bank account together on eight or nine occasions in 2023.

That story changed quickly.

Following the Dodgers' season-opening game against the San Diego Padres in South Korea, Mizuhara asked to address the team in the clubhouse. While the media was held out of the clubhouse—watching as the team's primary owner, Mark Walter, and Ohtani's agent, Nez Balelo, walked past—Mizuhara addressed the team and admitted to a gambling problem.

When reporters were allowed into the clubhouse, Ohtani was in a good mood, joking with a media relations staffer who tried to deter reporters from interviewing Ohtani about his Dodgers debut.

Ohtani agreed to the interview. Mizuhara was nowhere to be seen and Ohtani spoke for several minutes in Japanese to reporters from his home country. Mizuhara eventually appeared and translated a handful of questions for English-speaking reporters.

Ohtani later said he didn't fully understand what Mizuhara was saying when his interpreter addressed the team.

"In that meeting, he was speaking entirely in English," Ohtani said during a lengthy statement when the Dodgers returned to the United States. "I didn't have an interpreter and he spoke entirely in English so I couldn't fully understand what he was saying.... I was vaguely aware that something was amiss.

"At that time, he said to me he would like to talk about it in more detail after we returned to the hotel.... Of course, I didn't know Ippei had a gambling addiction nor did I know that he was in debt."

By the next morning in South Korea, Mizuhara's story of Ohtani covering his gambling debts willingly had fallen apart. He recanted, saying Ohtani had no knowledge of his gambling activities. Lawyers representing Ohtani accused his interpreter of "massive theft."

"In the course of responding to recent media inquiries, we discovered that Shohei has been the victim of a massive theft and we are turning the matter over to the authorities," Ohtani's lawyers said in a statement released March 20.

Mizuhara was immediately fired by the Dodgers, who declined comment on the situation.

"There's nothing to say. Literally nothing to say," Andrew Friedman said when approached by reporters before the second game in Seoul.

Dodgers manager Dave Roberts said there was no consideration given to keeping Ohtani out of the game that night, and Ohtani went 1-for-5 with a single, a sacrifice fly, and two more fly balls that came up just short of the wall in Gocheok Sky Dome.

It was a frenetic, anxiety-filled 24 hours for Dodgers team president and CEO Stan Kasten, who feared everything they had hoped to accomplish—on the field and off—with Shohei Ohtani in Dodger blue might go up in smoke.

Kasten had first heard from owner Mark Walter at 3:00 AM before the first game in Korea.

"He tells me what he had just been alerted to," Kasten recalled. "I'm going to say it was six to 12 hours—it might have been less than that—before I realized, 'Okay, this is not everything disappearing,' which was your first worry. All of this. [Kasten waves out toward Dodger Stadium from his office late in the 2024 season.] All of this? Was not ever going to happen. That was a worry but only for a few hours until we figured out the first version—which was still bad but not fatal for Shohei personally. He was helping a buddy. He never bet on anything. Okay, if that were the story, we can deal with that.

"But we were still trying to get to the bottom of things. Again, the first report we got was, 'A newspaper is about to write the following story.' We spent the day waiting and no story came out. So, wait—is this all bullshit? We didn't even know that for 24 to 36 hours, I think. Then we were informed, like, in the eighth inning of Game 1 [in Korea]—yeah, this is happening in the next hour. Which is why we all decided we don't want everyone to go home and be reading this and not know the facts. That's why we had the hurry-up, unrehearsed meeting in the locker room [after the game]."

By morning, though, the Dodgers were dealing with a different version of the story. Ohtani had not been helping a friend with a gambling debt. He had been robbed by that friend.

"Once there was Version 2, that didn't immediately allay any fears," Kasten said. "The first reaction was, 'Okay, what is going on here? Now we've heard two separate fucking versions of the story.' Remember, we had told the players in the locker room at 9:00 or 10:00 PM—between then and 7:00 in the morning, we had found out what was now the truth, but then was just known as Version 2.

"We had to go to every player at breakfast and say, 'Hey, what you heard last night? It's turned around.'... There was just a lot of confusion."

The news exploded in headlines across Japan and the United States.

Because of Ohtani's initial silence and Mizuhara's changing story, speculation ran rampant about Ohtani's involvement in his interpreter's gambling. Was Mizuhara just a front for Ohtani to gamble his millions? How could Mizuhara have such easy access to Ohtani's money? Why had Mizuhara changed his story? Was he being paid to take the fall for Ohtani?

Long-time baseball writer Hideki Okuda of *Sports Nippon* was working from his home in Osaka that spring when the news broke.

"I think it was the same as the United States—100 percent surprise," Okuda later said of the reaction in Japan. "Ippei Mizuhara became one of the idols [to Japanese fans]. Most of the people liked him. He was a good friend of Shohei Ohtani. His skill as an interpreter was very good. My son—born and raised in the United States [while Okuda was covering MLB]— he said [Mizuhara's] interpreting skills were one of the best. So people liked him."

With reporters now scrutinizing Mizuhara's life, some of his past claims unraveled. Mizuhara had said he graduated from the University of California–Riverside, but officials from the school said there were no records of anyone by that name attending the school.

The Angels' media guide during his years with the team said Mizuhara had worked as an interpreter for New York Yankees pitcher Hideki Okajima during spring training in 2012. There were also reports that Mizuhara had served as Okajima's interpreter during his time with the Boston Red Sox in 2010.

Neither appeared to be true, and the Red Sox even went so far as to release a statement saying Mizuhara had never worked for the team.

Within days of the blockbuster revelations, Major League Baseball announced that it had opened an investigation into "allegations involving Shohei Ohtani and Ippei Mizuhara."

By the time the Dodgers returned from Korea, Ohtani was secure enough that he knew what had happened to meet with five teammates—Freddie Freeman, Mookie Betts, Max Muncy, Tyler Glasnow, and Miguel Rojas—to answer their questions in a 45-minute private meeting. (Will Ireton was there to interpret.)

"It was him and them—not me, not Andrew [Friedman], not anybody else—and he laid out everything for them, talking to them," Kasten said. "They asked him questions. They were tough on him. And they all came out of there, saying, 'We got this. Now we understand.'"

Those players had been Ohtani's teammates for just a couple months. But they were predisposed to believe him, as teammates are, and ready to let him know they had his back going forward.

"We had our own questions and he answered our questions," Freeman said. "I believed that he had nothing to do with it. I'm always going to do that, no matter who it is. I'm going to believe you until I can't."

Two days later, Ohtani addressed the issue publicly for the first time, at a press conference at Dodger Stadium. Ohtani would not take questions and the expectation was that he would use the ongoing investigations (both criminal and MLB's) as an excuse to keep his comments brief without going into specifics.

But the statement he read in Japanese (translated by Ireton) was more expansive and went into much greater detail than expected during the approximately 12-minute monologue:

> Thank you everyone for coming. Over the past week or so, it's been a tough week for all the team members—the same goes for me—and for fans. I'm really grateful for your patience and understanding, including everyone in the media.

To begin with, I'm saddened, or rather shocked, by the mistake of someone I trusted—that's how I feel now. There's an ongoing investigation so please understand that there are limits to what I can say today. I've prepared some notes to convey what happened in plain terms so I'd like to follow those and explain what occurred.

Firstly, I have never engaged in gambling or bet on sports events on someone's behalf or asked someone to do that. And of course, I have never asked anyone to transfer money from my account to a bookmaker. Until a few days ago, I had no knowledge whatsoever that he [Ippei Mizuhara] was doing such things.

To sum things up, he stole money from my account and on top of that had lied to everyone including those around me. That's what it boils down to.

Last weekend in South Korea, my representatives received a message from the media asking if I was involved in illegal bookmaking or sports gambling. Ippei told everyone, including my representatives, that he paid the money to cover a certain friend's debt.

The next day, during further questioning, Ippei explained to my representatives that the debt was his own. That he had created it. He apparently told my representatives at that time that I had covered it. And these were all complete lies.

Ippei, of course, didn't inform me about the interview requests and he lied to the representatives that I had already talked and communicated with him. Yes, it was the same for me and the representatives and the team as well. He also lied to the representatives, saying that he had been communicating with me.

And the first time I learned of this issue regarding gambling was during the postgame team meeting held after the first game in South Korea. In that meeting, he was speaking entirely in English. I didn't have an interpreter and he spoke entirely in English so I couldn't fully understand what he was saying. Perhaps I could understand that he was saying something along those lines and I was vaguely feeling that something was amiss.

At that time, he said to me he would like to talk about it in more detail after we returned to the hotel and he asked me to wait, so at that time I decided to wait until we were at the hotel. At the time of the meeting, of course I didn't know that Ippei had a gambling addiction nor did I know that he was in debt.

I didn't agree to help him repay his debt at that time nor had I asked or authorized him to transfer money to a bookmaker. We went back to the hotel and talked with Ippei. That's when I found out that he had a massive debt.

He then told me that he had accessed my account without permission and transferred money to a bookmaker. I felt, "This is not right." So I called my representatives and we discussed the matter. After the discussion, my representatives learned for the first time that they had also been lied to by him and they immediately contacted the Dodgers and their lawyers.

It was then that both the Dodgers and my representatives learned for the first time that they had been lied to. The lawyers then reported that this was theft and fraud and that they would turn the matter over to the police.

This is the sequence of events. I am, of course, not involved in sports betting and there is absolutely no truth to me sending money to a bookmaker.

At this point, Ohtani looked up from his prepared notes and addressed the assembled media further (in Japanese with Ireton translating):

> I am beyond shocked. It's hard to verbalize how I am feeling at this point.
>
> How I've been feeling this entire week I can't put into words very well and it's hard for me to articulate it now.
>
> However, since the season is starting in full swing soon, I will let my lawyers take it from here and I also want to fully cooperate with the police. It's difficult to switch gears emotionally but I want to start again towards this season and I'm glad to be able to talk today.
>
> That's all I can say for now and I won't be taking any questions but I believe I'll continue to move forward from here. That's all. Thank you very much.

Two of Ohtani's Dodgers teammates, Joe Kelly and Kiké Hernández, stood in the back of the interview room. Team president Stan Kasten, manager Dave Roberts, GM Brandon Gomes, and president of baseball operations Andrew Friedman were also in the room.

"It was strong. It was powerful. It was unequivocal," Kasten later said of Ohtani's statement.

"He's handling this way better than I would," Hernández said. "Betrayal is hard…. We're human and [stuff] affects us in many different ways. He's doing a great job of not letting it [distract] him from what he needs to do on the field and his work."

Kelly agreed, saying Ohtani "handled it like a pro—better than I probably would."

Roberts spoke for most fans when he said Ohtani's statement had satisfied any lingering questions about his culpability in Mizuhara's gambling activity.

"For him to be able to collect his thoughts and speak honestly and openly and be very vulnerable was really huge," Roberts said. "I heard everything I needed to hear and I know the players feel the same way.

"I got a lot of questions answered as far as what he knew, what he didn't know, and I'm looking forward to just moving forward and letting the authorities take care of this."

While conspiracy lovers in the United States were not swayed by Ohtani's statement, most fans were satisfied by his version of events. As details from the ongoing federal investigation emerged, support for Ohtani's innocence in the matter grew—especially in Japan.

"Initially, yes, some people doubted [whether Ohtani was involved in gambling]," reporter Hideki Okuda said. "But there's a reason. We can't believe somebody who has that type of money has no idea some of his money is gone and he has no knowledge. And somebody who is so close to him was addicted to gambling? They spend almost 24 hours together. He has no idea? If you are a normal person, we cannot believe it.

"I feel the Japanese people felt the same way. But down the road, we learned the truth. We learned the truth from the court, the legal documents from the investigation. So we can believe his innocence."

By all accounts from his teammates, Ohtani didn't let the swirling scandal affect his demeanor or preparation for the season.

"The guy has been amazing in the clubhouse," veteran infielder Miguel Rojas said. "He's being professional, being quiet about it, and taking care of his stuff.

"I can't talk about what he's feeling but I can talk about being a teammate of his, and to see him go through that, it's a lot. I feel for the guy. All you can do is be here for him and support him."

That duty fell mostly on Ireton, the Dodgers employee who replaced Ippei Mizuhara as Ohtani's interpreter.

Well-liked by players, coaches, and staff alike, Ireton joined the Dodgers as the interpreter for pitcher Kenta Maeda during Maeda's first season in L.A., in 2016. Born in Tokyo, Ireton moved to the United States with his family at age 15 and played baseball at Occidental College and Menlo College, where he was the class valedictorian in 2012.

After internships with the Texas Rangers and New York Yankees, Ireton was hired to interpret for Maeda and quickly earned the nickname "Will the Thrill," for his effort while shagging fly balls during batting practice and a dugout dance used to inspire the team.

When Maeda left the Dodgers for the Minnesota Twins after the 2019 season, Ireton stayed with the organization as a player development coach with their Triple A team in Oklahoma City. After one season, he was back in Los Angeles as a performance operations manager for the big-league club, operating the sophisticated training and data-collection technology used by the team. That role quickly expanded, with Ireton intricately involved in compiling analytical information and scouting videos used in gameplanning.

But Mizuhara's gambling scandal and subsequent dismissal put Ireton back in the role of interpreter, even as he continued many of his gameplanning duties.

Dave Roberts quickly found the change positive, saying it was "difficult" at times having to go through Mizuhara for any communication with Ohtani. After six seasons in the United States, Ohtani speaks some English—more than he likes to let on to the media—and is able to communicate without constantly leaning on an interpreter when interacting with teammates and the coaching staff. With Ireton still fulfilling some of his other duties, Ohtani became more independent in the Dodgers' clubhouse than he was with Mizuhara constantly at his side in Anaheim.

"Actually, I would argue that it's going to help relations internally, because there's no longer a buffer," Roberts said of the change in interpreters. "I think that I've already seen it the last couple days. I think Shohei has been even more engaging with his teammates and I think there's only upside with that."

The players use a group chat to discuss things among themselves. When Ohtani first joined the team, it was Mizuhara who joined the group chat and often responded on Ohtani's behalf. Soon after the scandal broke and Mizuhara was dismissed, Ohtani began participating in the group chat himself.

"He speaks enough English to know he's got a good personality. He's fun to be around," Clayton Kershaw said of Ohtani. "All the extracurricular stuff, I feel like he handles it well because we don't notice it. I don't notice it."

Weeks later, Roberts said Ohtani had "blossomed" in Mizuhara's absence.

"He's become way more independent, way more open, which is ironic given that the person he trusted most deceived him," Roberts said at midseason. "We've seen his true personality come out."

Teammate Tyler Glasnow said during a podcast interview that "we all knew early on that Ippei was doing some shady stuff," and players informally let Ohtani know they had his back. Glasnow also said it seemed like Ohtani, remarkably, was never "very stressed about" the scandal.

"I think when you know that you've done nothing, it's just a matter of time before they figure it all out," Glasnow said on *The Chris Rose Rotation* podcast. "It seems like there has not been any mental sweat lost on his part, and I'm glad all this stuff has come out so he can focus. I'm sure he'll get asked about this all year but he'll handle it well."

And he did. Getting off to the best start of his career in the midst of the scandal, Ohtani had a powerful asset that helped him, team president Stan Kasten said.

"It is impressive as hell. But should we be surprised?" Kasten said later in the year. "We've seen how he performs under pressure. Did you see how he performed in the WBC last year? Did you see that? Did you sense any moment being too big for him? I did not.

"So it was not a surprise that he could manage it—especially because he was the one guy in the world who knew the truth from the start. He had no questions. He had no issues. He knew he hadn't done anything wrong. He knew he wasn't going to get in trouble.

"So I was not surprised that he came through it like that. Not surprised."

With so many reporters reacting to every twist and turn in the Ohtani-Mizuhara story, the potential for it to become a distraction for the rest of the Dodgers' clubhouse was strong. But Roberts dismissed that concern quickly.

"You have to be able to compartmentalize. You have to be a professional. And we have a lot of guys in that clubhouse that are professionals," the manager said as the Dodgers prepared to open the domestic portion of their schedule. "Not to say that they're not emotional, that they're not empathetic [to Ohtani's situation]. But we all have jobs to do.

"So for me, I wasn't concerned. Like I told you guys before, there's going to be distractions, as there always are off the field. But the core group of guys that we have—which now continues to grow, because we have that continuity—has weathered a lot of things.... We've got to focus on baseball and that's the only thing that guys are thinking about today, I promise you that."

For Ohtani, the loss was personal. Mizuhara was closer to him than anyone in his life, until his marriage to Mamiko Tanaka. Ohtani minimized the upheaval in his life, saying he was just "thankful that the team and the staff has supported me throughout the process."

As for his ability to focus on baseball?

"Regardless of whatever happens off the field, my ability to be able to play baseball hasn't changed," he said. "It is my job to make sure that I play to the best of my abilities."

While Ohtani adjusted to his new reality and new surroundings with the Dodgers, Ippei Mizuhara wound his way through the federal court system.

On April 12, he surrendered to federal authorities.

That night at Dodger Stadium, Ohtani was 3-for-5 with two doubles and a home run in an extra-innings loss to the San Diego Padres.

On May 8, Mizuhara reached an agreement to plead guilty to federal criminal charges for illegally transferring $17 million from Shohei Ohtani's account.

That afternoon, Ohtani went 0-for-4 in a 3–1 win over the Miami Marlins at Dodger Stadium.

On May 14, Mizuhara was in court to be arraigned on charges of bank fraud and filing a false tax return.

That night at Oracle Park, Ohtani went 3-for-5 with a home run and a double as the Dodgers routed the Giants, 10–2, in San Francisco. For the first—and possibly only—time, Ohtani really acknowledged how Mizuhara's betrayal had rocked his world, affecting his legendary ability to sleep.

"Initially, I really didn't have much sleep, obviously with the things that were happening," he said during that May series in San Francisco. "But now I've been able to really have a pretty consistent routine, being able to sleep well. I think that is leading to good results.

"As the incidents were progressing and the investigation was going on, as I was starting to not be involved anymore, that's when I was able to really focus on my sleep and being able to sleep better."

On June 4, Mizuhara appeared in court in Santa Ana and officially entered guilty pleas to the tax and bank fraud charges. The charges could bring a maximum sentence of 33 years in prison—though Mizuhara is expected to get a reduced sentence as part of the plea agreement.

Mizuhara spoke briefly in court while entering his pleas.

"I worked for Victim A [Ohtani] and I had access to his accounts," Mizuhara said. "I fell into gambling debt and the only way I could think of [to get out of debt] was to access his money. I wired money for my gambling debt from his account."

U.S. Attorney Martin Estrada spoke to reporters after the hearing, portraying Ohtani as vulnerable.

"Mr. Ohtani is an immigrant who came to this country, is not familiar with the ways of this country, and therefore was easily prey to someone who was more familiar with our financial systems," Estrada said.

Following the guilty pleas, Major League Baseball announced that it had closed its investigation into Ohtani's involvement.

"Based on the thoroughness of the federal investigation that was made public, the information MLB collected, and the criminal proceeding being resolved without being contested, MLB considers Shohei Ohtani a victim of fraud and this matter has been closed," MLB said in a statement released that day.

In a statement released by his representatives, Ohtani said Mizuhara's "full admission of guilt...has brought important closure to me and my family."

"This has been a uniquely challenging time, so I am especially grateful for my support team—my family, agent, agency, lawyers, and advisors, along with the entire Dodger organization, who showed endless support throughout this process," Ohtani's statement read.

"It's time to close this chapter, move on, and continue to focus on playing and winning ballgames."

That night, Ohtani was 1-for-4 as the Dodgers were shut out, 1–0, by the Pittsburgh Pirates.

"He's handled it with flying colors," Roberts said early in the season. "I just don't think it's going to affect performance. I really don't."

He was right.

Mizuhara was scheduled to be sentenced on December 20, 2024.

Chapter 4

Super Powers

Shohei Ohtani had not even suited up in a regular-season game for the Los Angeles Dodgers in 2024, and he was already demonstrating one of his super powers—sleeping.

At the press conference that followed the team's arrival in Seoul, South Korea, for the historic season-opening games against the San Diego Padres, Dodgers manager Dave Roberts revealed that Ohtani had led the team by sleeping 11 hours during the approximately 13-hour flight from Arizona to Korea.

It was the first of many impressive statistics Ohtani would produce in his initial season with the Dodgers.

For anyone who has followed Ohtani's career, however, it came as no surprise. Ohtani's ability and commitment to getting ample sleep has been part of his legend.

"Sleep is my top priority," he told Kyodo News in 2022, emphasizing that it is crucial to "a good recovery" after performing on the field, particularly after moving to MLB from the Japanese professional ranks, where both travel and scheduling are not as challenging.

Ohtani tries to get at least 10 hours of sleep each day, including fitting "power naps" into his workout schedule. One of his many endorsement deals has been with Japanese bedding maker Nishikawa, which customizes pillows for Ohtani with extra stuffing. Nishikawa even measured Ohtani with a 3-D body scanner to personalize its most expensive mattress model for him.

During his days with the Angels, Ohtani was known to travel with his own mattress as well as a weighted sleep mask. And Decoy, Ohtani's dog, even has his own custom-made dog bed, courtesy of Nishikawa.

When a well-rested Ohtani and the rest of the Dodgers arrived in Seoul, they were greeted at the airport by hundreds of fans, most wearing Dodgers gear and many waving "Shotime Korea" and "Goatani Go" signs. A beefed-up security detail followed the team every step of the way during their week in Korea.

"It's been a lot," Mookie Betts said of the traveling rock star treatment that came with being Ohtani's teammate. "But it's cool. It's kind of what comes when you get somebody like this [pointing to Ohtani], an international star."

The buzz created by Ohtani's visit to Korea led to more than 200 credentialed media covering the games at Gocheok Sky Dome in Seoul. But Freddie Freeman found the silver lining in all the added attention and media requests.

"When you have this kind of stuff going on, that means something exciting happened in the off-season," Freeman said upon arriving in Seoul. "When you sign Shohei, [Yoshinobu] Yamamoto, trade for Glas [Tyler Glasnow], sign him—just all the people we brought in. Mostly Sho. But this is because something really, really special happened in the off-season.

"I think we're kind of starting to get used to it a little bit. But I don't know if anybody can get used to this [pointing to the large crowd of reporters]. This is exciting. It's fun for us. It's fun to be playing in front of a lot more new fans this year."

Roberts reached into a different sport for a comparison, saying that traveling with the Ohtani Dodgers felt like what he imagined it must have been like traveling with Michael Jordan and the Chicago Bulls when they were atop the NBA.

"When we got to the airport, there were a lot of fans, a lot of media, and our players are very excited about that and I think it speaks to where the game of baseball is globally," Roberts said. "I think the interest, the excitement for Major League Baseball is at an all-time high. And for the Dodgers to be one of the teams to represent Major League Baseball here in Seoul is quite the honor."

It's a role the Dodgers have become familiar with over the franchise's history.

The trip to Korea was the second time they had opened the regular season on a different continent. In 2014, they played the first Major League Baseball games in Australia, playing two regular-season games against the Arizona Diamondbacks at the Sydney Cricket Ground.

Between that trip and the Seoul Series in 2024, they played a regular-season series in Monterrey, Mexico, against the San Diego Padres in 2018—a visit that included a combined no-hitter thrown by Walker Buehler and three relievers.

The Dodgers also made a five-game tour of Taiwan and Japan in 1993, played a historic exhibition game in Beijing, China, in March 2008, and then visited Taiwan again in 2010.

"This is an exciting part of baseball's effort to expand our reach globally, internationally," Dodgers team president Stan Kasten said on the eve of the trip to Korea. "We went to Australia in 2014. Teams go to London every year now, Mexico every year now. This year, we're also going to have programs in India, France, the D.R. [Dominican Republic]. We're also going to have games in the D.R. It's all part of that effort." (The Boston Red Sox and Tampa Bay Rays played two exhibition games in Santo Domingo in March 2024.)

In July 2024, it was announced that the Dodgers would be making more international history by opening a second consecutive season in Asia. They will play two exhibition games and two regular-season games against the Chicago Cubs at the Tokyo Dome in March 2025.

The Tokyo Series will bring four Japanese stars back home to play MLB games in front of their fans—Seiya Suzuki and Shōta Imanaga of the Cubs, Ohtani and Yamamoto of the Dodgers.

"If they do that, it'll be like traveling with a rock group. It will be," veteran Clayton Kershaw said when the prospect of a trip to Japan was still speculation. "It'll be an experience. It'll be something."

Still recovering from shoulder surgery in November 2023, Kershaw didn't make the trip to Korea in March 2024. For those who did, it was indeed an experience.

Many of the players and team staff took to it with gusto, touring places like Gyeongbokgung Palace and trying the variety of foods available at Myeongdong Night Market. The players' wives and girlfriends made the most of a visit to Olive Young, a renowned Korean health and beauty product chain. Pitchers Alex Vesia and Michael Grove sampled a series of Korean foods for a spot on television.

Glasnow called the atmosphere "very electric" once the Dodgers settled in at Gocheok Sky Dome for a workout and exhibition games against the Kiwoom Heroes and the Korean national team.

The Seoul Sky Dome has room for only about 16,000 fans—a far cry from the 50,000-plus of Dodger Stadium (or the 55,000 likely to fill the Tokyo Dome for the Dodgers' visit in 2025). But the gameday atmosphere was augmented by cheer squads pounding drums—their clothes coordinated to the two visiting MLB teams—and dance routines performed on platforms set up on either side of the stands with personalized songs for individual players.

The cheerleaders danced to K-pop songs between innings, and pitching changes were accompanied by special effects from the lighting system. South Korean actress Jeon Jong-seo threw out the first pitch before one game—drawing the rapt attention of players in both dugouts. Their admiration for the actress was caught on video and was briefly a popular online highlight.

"In between innings or while the inning is going on, the songs and the sounds and stuff...it's really cool," Glasnow said. "I hope we can adopt that back home. It's great. It's been really cool."

Glasnow noted how "you can tell everyone's locked into the game—no one's on their phone and looking around"—a slight slap at the average American fan's ability to be distracted.

Roberts called it "a different environment" from MLB games in the United States and praised the Korean fans for how they "kept their energy up throughout the whole night."

"I don't think they knew in left field that the game had ended," Roberts joked after one of the exhibition games. "It's one of those things where we don't get a chance to experience other cultures of baseball. So to have cheerleaders out in left field and right field or down the lines is something different."

The Dodgers enjoyed themselves on the field as well, pounding the Kiwoom Heroes, 14–3, and beating the Korean national team, 5–2, in their two final tune-ups before the season-opening games against the Padres.

Ohtani went hitless in the two exhibition games. In the game against the Korean national team, he batted twice and struck out twice against Ariel Jurado, a Panamanian right-hander who had some big-league experience. In his 45 MLB games—44 in the American League West with the Texas Rangers, and one with the New York Mets—Jurado held Ohtani, then the Angels DH, to two hits in 11 at-bats (.182). When he struck Ohtani out twice in Korea, it briefly made Jurado the man of the moment.

"He's great. He's the best player in the major leagues," Jurado said. "I think I used the same sequence like when I was in the major leagues—some fastballs up. He swung—thank you for me."

Ohtani had better luck when the games counted.

In his second official at-bat as a Dodger, he got his first hit of the new season, a single to right field off fellow countryman Yu Darvish in the season opener against the Padres.

Typical of Ohtani, it was not an ordinary single, and the at-bat demonstrated another of his super powers—the ability to hit a baseball harder and more consistently than almost anyone in the game.

In his third-inning at-bat against Darvish, Ohtani drove a high fly ball down the right-field line that went foul. It left the bat at 119.2 mph. Only two players hit a ball harder in MLB all season—Oneil Cruz of the Pittsburgh Pirates (121.5 and 120.4 mph) and Giancarlo Stanton of the New York Yankees (120 mph).

Two pitches later, Ohtani ripped his single to right at 112.3 mph—prompting his wife, Mamiko, to exchange high-fives with her neighbors in the Dodgers' family seating section (as shown on TV).

Exit velocity statistics—as well as other analytical data such as spin rates, barrel accuracy, and launch angles—are a product of Statcast, an automated tool developed to track and analyze player movements as well as pitch characteristics and batted balls. The highly sophisticated system was introduced to all Major League Baseball stadiums in 2015—now known as the beginning of the "Statcast Era."

The technology uses a high-speed camera system known as Hawk-Eye for pitch tracking, hit tracking, player tracking, and bat tracking during all MLB games. The Hawk-Eye system (the same system used for instant replay at professional tennis tournaments) was added in 2020. Each stadium now has 12 Hawk-Eye cameras arrayed around the field. Five are 300 frames-per-second cameras that focus on bat and pitch tracking. The rest track player movement and batted balls, allowing 99 percent coverage of batted balls. During the 2023 season, over 725,000 pitches and 125,000 batted balls were tracked and quantified by Statcast.

The statistics are now an omnipresent part of baseball coverage. In the case of exit velocity, anything that leaves the bat at 95 mph or higher is considered a hard-hit ball. Ohtani's 112.3 mph single in Seoul was the first of 288 balls he would put in play with exit velocities over 95 mph during the 2024 season, the most in MLB.

"He's in a class by himself," Dave Roberts said. "His average exit velocity on balls he puts in play is—he's got to be in a category by himself. The ball just does different things when it comes off his bat."

Veteran left-hander Clayton Kershaw, still recovering from his shoulder surgery in November 2023, donned a headset and joined a SportsNet LA broadcast from the dugout during an early season game. He was impressed by Ohtani's ability to hit the ball harder more consistently than anyone he'd ever seen.

"This is unbelievable," Kershaw said on the SNLA broadcast. "Every ball that he hits is—he's just so strong. I don't get it. I don't think anybody does know how he does it. It's just amazing.

"We have some guys who can hit the ball pretty hard. But I think consistently what he can do is pretty amazing. The balls that he's hitting 115, 118, 120 [mph]—there's not too many guys around the game that can do that."

Dodgers first baseman Freddie Freeman said the same, calling Ohtani's ability to hit the ball hard "pretty amazing."

"He seems to hit the ball over 105 mph every single time he hits the ball," Freeman said. "He's just special."

It's a special talent that puts Ohtani in a small class of sluggers pretty much confined to Ohtani, Aaron Judge, Giancarlo Stanton, and Pirates shortstop Oneil Cruz. Judge led all MLB hitters in 2024 with an average exit velocity of 96.2 mph. Ohtani was second at 95.8 mph, followed by Cruz (95.5) and Stanton (94.6).

"He uses his body super-efficiently," explained Dodgers hitting coach Robert Van Scoyoc. "He creates a ton of stretch in his core, shoulders, and wrist. Obviously it's a ton of speed and leverage built into his body."

Dave Roberts has been in the game as a player, coach, and manager for the past 25 years. By midseason, he had run out of ways to describe Ohtani's hard-hit balls.

"Honestly, the way the ball comes off [hit bat]—I've never seen anything like it," said Roberts. "I haven't seen Stanton a lot. I played with Barry Bonds and the ball just didn't come off like it does on Shohei's bat. And Barry might be the greatest hitter of all time. But what Shohei does, how hard the ball comes off, it's just different than anything I've ever seen."

Ohtani's first hit as a Dodger was one of few highlights through the first seven innings of that season opener in Seoul. The Dodgers went into the eighth inning trailing the Padres, 2–1, before putting together a four-run rally to come from behind and win the game.

Two walks and a single by Teoscar Hernández loaded the bases with no outs. A sacrifice fly by Kiké Hernández tied the game before an odd play put the Dodgers on top.

Gavin Lux bounced an easy ground ball to the right side of the infield, where Padres first baseman Jake Cronenworth seemed poised to start an inning-ending double play. But the ball broke through the webbing of his glove and bounced through. The go-ahead run scored on the play, a rare error charged for "equipment failure."

After the ball broke through, so did the Dodgers. Mookie Betts and Ohtani followed with RBI singles and the Dodgers won the historic opening game, 5–2.

"The biggest thing is that we got the 'W' and the way we got it, coming back late in the game like that, proves that we're a really good team," Ohtani said after going 2-for-5 with a stolen base and that RBI in his Dodgers debut.

There had been no concerns voiced by the Dodgers, but Ohtani's spring results and his hitless exhibition games in Seoul had been unimpressive, and his swing didn't look ready for the season.

The first of his 61 multi-hit games in 2024 assuaged that fear.

"Sometimes with hitters, one swing gets you back," Roberts said, pointing to the 119.2-mph foul ball. "Even in spring, he was getting some hits. But I really feel that one swing where he pulled it in the air foul, he really took a good swing and I think that bled into that at-bat where he lined a ball into right field for a hit and had another big base hit later in the game."

The good feelings—and the Dodgers' unbeaten record—were washed away in the next 24 hours.

By the morning after the season opener, Ohtani's interpreter, Ippei Mizuhara, had admitted to a gambling addiction and been fired by the Dodgers amid allegations of "massive theft" from Ohtani to cover his gambling debts.

"We're here to play baseball," Dave Roberts said before the second game against the Padres. "Obviously with what happened yesterday, we did a good job of focusing on a baseball game and we're going to do the same thing today."

Roberts dismissed the idea that the turmoil created by Mizuhara might prompt him to take Ohtani out of the lineup for the second game—or that Ohtani might not want to play.

Ohtani did not address the media before the game nor did he take the field for the Dodgers' pregame workout. That is not unusual. Ohtani rarely takes batting practice on the field, preferring to do his work in the batting cages.

"Shohei is ready," Roberts said. "I know that he's preparing in the hitters' meeting right now and he'll be ready to play in tonight's game."

Ohtani was ready. Yoshinobu Yamamoto was not.

In his Dodgers debut, Yamamoto did nothing to justify the record $325 million contract the Dodgers had given him. The first four Padres batters he faced reached base and scored. Yamamoto needed 43 pitches to retire three batters. He gave up five runs and was done for the day after that one inning.

The bad first impression created doubts about Yamamoto's ability to handle the challenges of transitioning to Major League Baseball.

But he wasn't alone in struggling through that game. The Dodgers and Padres combined to use 13 pitchers. Only three of those pitchers—Yuki Matsui and Robert Suárez for the Padres and Gus Varland for the Dodgers—didn't give up a run, and they were around for just two outs each.

The Dodgers added two errors to the messy game and lost 15–11 despite Mookie Betts driving in six runs with four hits—including the first home run of the Seoul Series. Ohtani showed no evidence of being unsettled by the events off the field and went 1-for-5 with another single, another RBI, and his first run scored as a Dodger.

"On the offensive side—a lot of good things," Roberts said. "On the pitching side, it just wasn't very good. Across the board, we just didn't execute. I think eight, nine walks in there. And defensively, we weren't good either."

Having split the two historic games in Korea, the Dodgers boarded their plane home with a 1–1 record, looking nothing like the "super team" of the hyperbolic winter and shadowed by the developing story surrounding Ohtani and Mizuhara.

"It's been a long week but there are no excuses," Betts said. "It's been a great experience. It's been awesome being here and getting a chance to see a new culture.

"But it is what it is. You have to show up no matter the cards you're dealt."

The schedule gave the Dodgers a week off once they returned from Korea, allowing them to re-acclimate after the time change before opening the domestic part of their schedule. It also gave time for doubts about their championship potential to spread. Yamamoto's poor performance, some defensive shortcomings in the Seoul Series games, and, of course, the looming distraction of the Mizuhara scandal fueled the doubters but did not dissuade the Dodgers' decision-makers.

"I think to extrapolate a whole bunch of things from two games doesn't seem like the wisest thing to do," GM Brandon Gomes said. "It's still a really talented team. I don't feel any different than I did going into those two games in Korea."

As for the possibility that Ohtani's off-field drama might affect the Dodgers in the clubhouse or on the field, president of baseball operations Andrew Friedman was quick to dismiss any concern.

"I am not worried about that," he said.

The Dodgers have had their share of off-field issues in recent seasons.

Sexual assault allegations led to Trevor Bauer being suspended by MLB and eventually released by the Dodgers in 2021. In 2023, a second domestic violence issue also led to Julio Urías being removed from the team. During his days with the Dodgers, Yasiel Puig also generated his share of off-field drama.

"I think we're certainly battle-tested in that regard," Dodgers manager Dave Roberts said of dealing with Ohtani's situation. "We've shown over the years that we continue to move forward. Not to be insensitive to various situations, but we all understand we have jobs to do. And so, first and foremost, playing baseball and preparing [for the season] has to be a priority."

Big-leaguers, and athletes in general, "have a very good ability to compartmentalize," Roberts said.

"I think that's just kind of how we're wired," he said. "That's kind of what baseball players do."

They went back to doing what they do, beating the Los Angeles Angels, 5–3, at Dodger Stadium in the first game of the annual preseason Freeway Series.

Suiting up in a Dodgers uniform at Dodger Stadium for the first time, Ohtani batted three times, going 0-for-2 with a walk and a strikeout against his former team.

Ohtani took his biggest swing the next day, delivering that 12-minute statement in which he denied any involvement in gambling and put all the blame on Mizuhara for lying and stealing millions of dollars from him.

Hours after reading his statement and seeming to put many of the questions aside, Ohtani and his new teammates played another exhibition game against his old team. Ohtani once again went hitless.

Two nights later, he was back on the field at Angel Stadium, this time wearing the blue uniform of the Los Angeles Dodgers for the third and final game of the Freeway Series. A video tribute played on the scoreboards as Ohtani walked to the plate for his first at-bat as a visitor in Anaheim.

A two-time MVP and two-way sensation during his six years with the Angels, Ohtani tipped his helmet and bowed to both sides of the stadium as the fans cheered, expressing their appreciation for those years and memories.

Then Ohtani swung and missed at Chase Silseth's fastball, striking out to start another hitless game. Whether the distraction of Ippei Mizuhara's revelations were a factor or just fatigue from the Dodgers' globe-trotting, Ohtani was 0-for-6 with three strikeouts and two walks in the final three tune-ups before the regular season.

"When we were in South Korea, I thought he swung the bat really well," Dave Roberts said. "These last three games, he just hasn't synced up, but I'm sure he'll be ready to go on Thursday."

Thursday, March 28, was a big day for Dodgers fans. Opening Day always is. But the anticipation for this home opener was elevated by the off-season acquisitions of Shohei Ohtani,

Yoshinobu Yamamoto, and Tyler Glasnow (who would start the game), and intensified by waiting through the trip to Korea—games that were played in the middle of the night in California.

They rolled out the "blue carpet" for the home opener, introducing the players individually as they trotted in through the center-field wall and to the home dugout—a fairly long trip as pregame introductions go. Ohtani's introduction was greeted with a loud ovation from the sold-out crowd of 52,667.

"I felt the walk was a little too long," Ohtani joked after the game. "But I thought the ceremony was well done."

Being on the opposite side in front of a full house at Dodger Stadium was a new experience for Ohtani, who had played there frequently with the Angels; they had lost their last six games there through the 2023 season.

"I'm very grateful, now being part of the Dodgers and being received by the Dodger fans," Ohtani said. "Obviously I've been here before as an opposing player so it was a little intimidating. I'm very grateful for the fans—and there were a lot of them."

Those fans roared with approval when Ohtani's name was announced before his first at-bat against Cardinals starter Miles Mikolas. The power of the moment might have gotten to Ohtani. With Betts on first base, Ohtani shot a double into right field. Third-base coach Dino Ebel held Betts at third—but Ohtani kept running and was tagged out before he could get back to second base.

Ohtani took blame for the blunder, saying he hadn't looked for Ebel soon enough and would "make the adjustment" in the future.

"He can run very fast but he's got to understand there's a guy in front of him too," Roberts said. "It was certainly a stand-up triple [if he could have kept running]. But when you've got Freddie [Freeman] behind him, you don't want to make that first out at home plate [by sending Betts]. So you've got to keep your head up too."

It didn't slow the Dodgers down. They scored twice in the first inning. In the third, Betts and Freeman hit home runs with an Ohtani walk in between. The Dodgers rolled to a 7–1 victory.

Ohtani reached base for a third time in the game when he ripped a single to right field in the fifth inning. The single left his bat with an exit velocity of 113.9 mph, the hardest-hit ball by a Dodger since 2021.

The Dodgers took six of seven games from the St. Louis Cardinals and the San Francisco Giants on that first homestand, with Betts and Ohtani leading the way from the top of the Dodgers' three-MVP lineup.

Despite the challenge of moving to shortstop—a position he hadn't played regularly since high school—late in spring training, Betts was off to an MVP-level start. Including the games in Korea, Betts had five home runs in the Dodgers' first nine games while batting .485 (16-for-33), driving in 11 runs, and scoring 14.

By comparison, Ohtani was off to a modest start with his new team. He ended the first homestand with a .270 batting average (10-for-37) with four RBIs and seven runs, scored—but he had a major-league-leading nine batted balls with exit velocities of 100 mph or higher.

"I feel like I'm seeing the ball well," Ohtani said. "But I feel like there's a little bit something off with my timing and being able to kind of feel the distance between the ball and myself."

Things didn't get better until his last at-bat of the homestand, when Ohtani hit his first home run as a Dodger. The 430-foot drive came in the seventh inning off Giants lefty reliever Taylor Rogers—and set off a little controversy when it landed in the right-field pavilion at Dodger Stadium.

The ball wound up in the hands of Amber Roman, who described herself as a diehard Dodgers fan. Roman and her husband, Alex Valenzuela, were escorted from their seats by stadium security. This is the usual approach when a milestone ball finds its way into the stands, with team officials offering to make a trade for the ball so that the player involved can have it as a souvenir.

Roman and Valenzuela said there were always willing to give the ball back to Ohtani but were unhappy with what they said team officials offered in exchange—two signed caps. With nearby fans chiming in, team officials eventually got Roman to accept two signed caps, a signed ball, and a signed bat from Ohtani. Still, it was a far cry from the estimated $100,000— perhaps inflated by the moment—that Ohtani's first home run ball as a Dodger could have drawn at a memorabilia auction.

A week later, when the Dodgers returned from a road trip, the Dodgers made good. Roman and Valenzuela were escorted to the Dodgers clubhouse and met Ohtani personally. Roman posted photos with Ohtani on social media with the caption "Best Birthday Ever!!"

For Ohtani, the first home run in his 41st plate appearance as a Dodger was a relief.

"My feeling of 'I want to hit one quickly, I want to hit one quickly' was moving me away from taking good at-bats," Ohtani said. "[Manager Dave Roberts] told me, 'Just continue to be yourself.' That made me feel relaxed."

Ohtani stayed relaxed and even got hot on a chilly road trip to Chicago and Minnesota. On a windy 43-degree day at Wrigley Field on April 5, he went 2-for-5 with a double and his second home run.

He was on base three times (two singles and a walk) the next day, and had a double and a triple as the Dodgers took the series with a 8–1 win on April 7.

The cold weather followed the Dodgers to Minnesota, and so did Ohtani's surge at the plate. After going 6-for-13 in the three games at Wrigley Field, he had two doubles and another home run in the first game at Target Field. Ohtani credited his 9-for-18 binge to "several adjustments in the [batting] cage" and "some drills to improve my mechanics." That it followed the breakthrough of his first home run before leaving town was not a coincidence, he said.

"Yes, I do believe just getting the first one out of the way really helped mentally," he said.

One of those drills was an unusual one, a spur-of-the-moment choice as the Dodgers sat out a rain delay during the final game at Wrigley Field. The Dodgers travel with "a bunch of toys" in their hitting bags, assistant hitting coach Aaron Bates said, and Ohtani grabbed a bat with a flat barrel, similar to a cricket bat, and started hitting off a tee with it.

"Everyone was delirious at that point, when it's a rain delay, kind of messing around and stuff," Bates said of the nearly three-hour wait. "And then I think all the guys started using it after he did."

Since Ohtani had success in the games that followed, "then it works, I guess," Bates joked.

The Dodgers returned home with a 10–5 record to start their season and Ohtani on a tear. That tear continued in the first game of a series against their Seoul-mates, the San Diego Padres. Ohtani was 3-for-5 with two doubles and his fourth home run of the season. Batting .270 when the Dodgers left town, Ohtani was now batting .353 with a 1.098 OPS on the way to the best start of his career as a hitter.

But the Dodgers lost two out of three games to the Padres, did the same against the Washington Nationals, and then lost the first two games of a series against the New York Mets—a 2–6 slide at home that dropped them to 12–11 to start the season.

The Dodgers would not be the first team to open a season overseas and start slowly after the disruption—the early start and compressed schedule of spring training, traveling, and changing time zones. In fact, the Dodgers themselves were just 23–22 after the first 45 games of the 2014 season, when they opened with two games in Australia.

Injuries—specifically to pitchers—were an issue then and would prove to be once again in 2024. Clayton Kershaw started on Opening Day then missed the next five weeks of the 2014 season with a muscle injury in the back of his shoulder (then came back to win both the National League Cy Young and Most

Valuable Player awards that year). Six starting pitchers would be among the major-league-leading 15 players on the Injured List at the All-Star break in 2024.

"When we lose this many games like this, it's not the best atmosphere, but we're doing our very best to make sure we're moving on and do our best in our next game," Ohtani said during the 2–7 slide. "I'm sure there's a little bit of frustration. But it's also our ability to be able to move on and learn from it and be able to take advantage of it in future opportunities."

The homestand ended with the Dodgers—and Ohtani—on an upswing. He hit a two-run home run on April 21 to drive in the first runs in a 10–0 victory over the New York Mets. The home run was the 176th of Ohtani's career, moving him past Hideki Matsui for the most home runs hit in MLB by a Japanese-born player.

"Honestly, I'm relieved and happy. It took a while to get to this point since my last homer, so I'm just honestly happy and relieved," said Ohtani. "[The record for Japanese-born players] is not something I was cognizant of when I first started my career here. But as I've gotten to know where he was, then yes [it became a goal]."

The goal-oriented Ohtani had another target to shoot for early in the season.

It became a tongue-in-cheek point in the media when it emerged that Dave Roberts—born in Okinawa, Japan, to a Japanese mother and American father—held the Dodgers' franchise record for home runs by a Japanese-born player.

Roberts' total of seven home runs in 302 games with the Dodgers put him at the top of a list of Japanese-born sluggers that included pitchers Hideo Nomo (four home runs while with the Dodgers), Kenta Maeda (one), Kazuhisa Ishii (one)—and no one else.

When Ohtani hit home runs in three consecutive games from May 4–6 against the Atlanta Braves and Miami Marlins, he blew past Roberts for the record like a Porsche passing traffic on the highway.

As the franchise record became a running joke, Juan Toribio of MLB.com asked the Dodgers manager if he expected Ohtani to gift him a Porsche—a reference to the car Ohtani gave to Joe Kelly's wife, Ashley, for her part in getting Joe to give up his uniform number when Ohtani signed with the Dodgers.

Roberts jokingly said he hoped to receive a car from Ohtani as compensation for losing his home run record.

"He said he wanted a car," Ohtani said after the game when he passed Roberts. "I'm glad he's happy. He got a car."

Roberts interrupted the press conference to show reporters the toy Porsche Ohtani had given him.

"I just want to say congratulations and thank you very much," Roberts said, smiling broadly and laughing as he held up his small replica Porsche. "This is my car. The difference is Joe's car doesn't fit in my office. This car fits on my desk."

Reporters asked what it might take for Roberts to earn a real Porsche.

"If we win the World Series, I'll think about it," Ohtani said, playing along with the joke.

According to Roberts, the prank was just the most public example of how Ohtani was enjoying his new life with the Dodgers.

"I think with Shohei, it just speaks to how comfortable he feels here with the Dodgers, how excited he is to play winning baseball," the Dodgers manager said. "Arguably [Ohtani] has a chance to be one of the great players of our generation, if not beyond, but ultimately guys are competitors and they want to play for a championship. And so, I think the way he's been received, the way he's melded with our ballclub, how much the fans have embraced him—he feels it. He feels it and I do believe that it translates into performance and I think he's having as much fun as he's ever had."

Individually, Ohtani might have been off to the best start of his career offensively. But he started just 1-for-19 with runners in scoring position, perhaps trying too hard to make a good impression on his new teammates, expanded fan base, and $700 million employers.

"I think that he wants to be 'the guy,'" Roberts said by way of diagnosis. "I think that at certain times, you want to be 'the guy' and they [opposing teams] don't want him to beat them. So there's an expansion of the strike zone and he's just got to continue to be disciplined in the strike zone. That's the challenge for a guy who is a really aggressive swinger."

During Ohtani's April struggles with runners on base, Roberts said he had a conversation with Ohtani about how pitchers were taking advantage of his aggressiveness and "I thought he was expanding [the strike zone] a little bit more than he needed to."

"Some [pitchers] try to crowd him. Some try to go up [above the strike zone]. Some try to spin him [with breaking pitches]," Roberts said. "It just boils down to…if you control the strike zone, swing at strikes—but with Shohei there's just going to be more damage."

That became an ongoing theme with Ohtani throughout the season—when he resisted the temptation to swing at pitches outside of his best hitting zones, he had his greatest success. When he didn't—particularly with runners on base—he would get himself out.

"The zone I am swinging in is a little bit larger with runners in scoring position," Ohtani acknowledged at one point. "With nobody on base, I'm pretty good at it [plate discipline]. So it's just widening down the zone and, yes, we talked about it with Doc."

Given Ohtani's ability to cover so much of the strike zone and hit so many different pitches hard, it was not always an easy line to draw.

"He's a guy that can hit a lot of pitches, and at times he likes to test the limits of what he can hit and can't hit," Dodgers hitting coach Robert Van Scoyoc said. "But it's helping him understand it doesn't really matter who you are, you're going to have more success in the strike zone. Also, it makes him a tougher out. It doesn't give them a 'Get Out of Jail Free' card to beat him. If he's able to stay in the strike zone, he's dangerous. Aggression is also dangerous, too, so it's a double-edged sword. When he's swinging the bat, yeah, they can get him out outside the zone. But they also know they've got to make a really good pitch too.

"So I think it works both ways. Kind of for everything you do, there are attacks. If you're too aggressive, you chase. Too passive, you leave stuff on the table and maybe pitchers get comfortable. Like anything, there's a balance to it."

Ohtani found that balance often enough to hit .317 (40-for-126) with runners in scoring position after that 1-for-19 start. His batting average (.326) in situations determined to be "Late/Close" was one of the best in MLB for the 2024 season, despite that rough start with runners in scoring position. (Late and Close situations are a statistical designation created by STATS Inc. Defined as the seventh inning or later with the team at bat leading by one run or in a tie game or with the potential tying run on base, at bat, or on deck.)

"It's just regardless of the situation, just sticking to my approach no matter what," Ohtani said of his approach with runners on base. "That's more of the change I did—which is no change."

Chapter 5

Sushi...or Pizza?

When Shohei Ohtani hit the 176th home run of his career, passing Hideki Matsui for the most by a Japanese-born player in MLB history, it put the first runs on the board in a 10–0 Dodgers victory over the New York Mets.

That runaway win on Sunday, April 21, at Dodger Stadium, ended a poor homestand on a positive note and sent the Dodgers off on their longest road trip of the season—a 5,700-mile international affair that took them to Washington, D.C., Toronto, and then Phoenix.

It also started the best stretch of their 2024 season. The win over the Mets was the Dodgers' first of 17 victories over the next 21 games. They had been one game over .500 (12–11) and one game up in a National League West filled with teams with losing records. Twenty-one games later, they were 14 games over .500 (29–15) and 7½ games up in the division—a cushion that would sustain them through some rough stretches ahead.

The 21-game surge was led by the three former MVPs atop the Dodgers' lineup. Mookie Betts' early power burst had slowed but he hit .333 during the 17–4 stretch with an .881 OPS while playing the unfamiliar position of shortstop. The combination stamped Betts as an early frontrunner—alongside Ohtani—for another MVP award.

Freddie Freeman had started the season slowly but began putting it together during this stretch, batting .312 with 13 RBIs, 14 runs scored, and a .967 OPS.

But it was Ohtani whose dynamic performance led the way. He hit .364 with eight home runs, 19 RBIs, 17 runs scored, and a 1.177 OPS during the Dodgers' run, springing to the front of the MVP race.

Ohtani reached the 25-game mark of his first season with the Dodgers leading the majors in hard-hit balls (exit velocity of 95 mph or higher), with 50; hard-hit percentage (61.7 percent); and the highest single exit velocity of the season to that point (118.7 mph).

Through April 24 (26 games), he was off to the best start of his career, leading the majors in batting average (.371), hits (39), extra-base hits (21), runs scored (22), total bases (73), on-base percentage (.433), slugging percentage (.695), and OPS (1.129).

It was all more than the Dodgers expected given the significant changes in Ohtani's baseball life—a new team, a surgically repaired and still-rehabbing elbow—and the distractions off the field involving his former translator, Ippei Mizuhara.

"It's remarkable, obviously, the recovery and the work he's put in," Roberts said. "With Shohei, it's not just the slug, it's how hard he consistently hits the baseball. I can't imagine a player hitting it that often that hard consistently. That's what's remarkable to me.... Everything he hits, it seems like it's 110 [mph] off the bat—versus left [-handed pitching], versus right.

"From where he was a year ago [with elbow surgery] to be where he is right now is truly remarkable."

The Dodgers' long road trip began with one of Ohtani's more "remarkable" swings of the season—a ninth-inning home run at Nationals Park on April 23.

Ohtani ripped a hanging slider from Nationals reliever Matt Barnes 118.7 mph off the bat. It traveled an estimated 450 feet deep into the upper deck at Nationals Park in the blink of an eye—and stunned even his teammates.

"It looked like a cruise missile," Dodgers outfielder James Outman said after the game. "That was absurd. That was just absurd."

At 118.7 mph, it was the hardest-hit ball of Ohtani's career and the hardest-hit ball by any Dodgers player since Statcast began tracking exit velocities, in 2015. "It was a top-spin liner that reached the second deck," Roberts said of the homer. "There's not too many guys that can do that. It's lightning in that bat."

Dodgers third baseman Max Muncy also found it astonishing that Ohtani hit the ball an estimated 450 feet with top spin. Balls hit with top spin do not usually carry as far.

"The farthest top-spin ball I've ever seen in my life," Muncy marveled. "To hit a ball in the upper deck with top spin is pretty impressive.

"If he hit that with back spin, it's out of the stadium for sure."

In his first at-bat the next day, Ohtani ripped a double off the center-field wall that left his bat at 115.6 mph. It was the first of three doubles he had in the 11–2 rout and the first of five balls he put in play that day, all with exit velocities of 95 mph or higher.

"I have more time in general, so there's benefit to that," Ohtani said of the connections being drawn between his getting off to the best start of his career while performing only as a hitter. "But at the same time…I am preparing the same way I've been preparing, in a sense. That hasn't changed. But it's much easier to be able to maintain my conditioning without having to put a lot of effort into the pitching side."

Working with Ohtani every day, Dodgers hitting coach Robert Van Scoyoc saw some elements Ohtani brought from the pitching side into his hitting preparation.

"He's really consistent. He has his check points he wants to hit throughout the day with his bat speed and stuff," Van Scoyoc said. "I think he brings a lot of the pitching world into hitting in terms of measuring his process—something the hitting world is lagging behind. Pitching is a closed loop. Hitting is not. So it's not always as much a one-to-one. It's also harder to measure hitting than pitching. TrackMan captures a lot more of the pitching process than it does for hitting. We get the outcome."

TrackMan is a digital technology used by most professional teams. It employs Doppler radar and cameras to track a ball from the moment it is released by a pitcher to the end of a play, providing a variety of metrics including spin rate, vertical approach angle, exit speed, and launch angle.

"TrackMan doesn't capture the bat yet," Van Scoyoc said. "So until you get the bat and all the angles off the bat, you're going to be a step behind [relative to pitching]. It's not going to be the same. You're not going to be able to capture all of the ingredients like you would with a pitcher."

Ohtani is "more regimented than a lot of players" in the way he uses that data as a hitter, Van Scoyoc said.

"It seems like when he was doing the pitching and hitting, he wanted measurables," the coach said. "So he brought some of that into the cage."

After sweeping three games from the Nationals, the Dodgers moved on to Toronto—finally putting Ohtani on a plane to Canada (as had been erroneously reported in December as his free agency wound down).

Ohtani acknowledged that he had given serious consideration to signing with the Blue Jays in December. But he was shocked to hear reports that he had actually done so.

"In regards to the off-season, I was as surprised as any fans, in terms of the news that was going around," Ohtani said on the eve of the April trip north of the border. "But I did meet with the Blue Jays organization. And the impression that I got was it was a really, really great organization. The fans are really good. The city too. So I'm really looking forward to going to Toronto."

Blue Jays fans were looking forward to it as well—in December and April.

A sold-out crowd of 39,688 filled Rogers Centre for Ohtani's first visit with the Dodgers, and the fans behaved like so many jilted lovers. They booed Ohtani when his name was announced and he stepped to the plate for his first at-bat in the series opener on April 26.

Rising to the moment, Ohtani responded by hitting a home run. And got booed some more.

"After he homered, the guys in the dugout booed him as well," Dave Roberts said. "That was pretty funny. He got a big kick out of that."

Ohtani also seemed slightly amused by the fans' voicing their disapproval so loudly—as if he somehow was responsible for the false reports in the media.

"Not surprised," Ohtani said with a laugh after the game when he was asked about being booed. "I really do feel that the fans here are passionate and when they are, that's the kind of reception that they will probably do. So I'm just very grateful and respectful that the fans here are passionate just as much as the Dodgers fans are with us."

Ohtani once again said he was "very grateful for the teams that approached me and wanted to sign me."

"Ultimately I could only choose one team," he said.

Ohtani went quiet after his homer as the Dodgers pounded out 19 hits in a 12–2 win. He drove in another run in the second game of the series before his team dropped the finale.

The road trip concluded in Arizona with a three-game rematch against the Diamondbacks team that eliminated the Dodgers in shocking fashion from the 2023 postseason.

The Dodgers took two of three this time, denying that revenge was on their minds. Along the way, the series featured one of the strangest games of the season.

On April 30, the Dodgers and Diamondbacks were preparing for the second game of the series when a swarm of bees began gathering atop the screen behind home plate.

"I got a call about five minutes before game time from our senior manager of events. She doesn't usually call me about that time, so I knew something was odd," Diamondbacks vice president of ballpark operations Mike Rock said. "She said, 'We have bees landing on the net right behind home plate.' I said, 'How many?' She said, 'Hundreds. No wait—thousands.' And I knew we had a problem."

A call went out to Matt Hilton of Blue Sky Pest Control. Hilton was at his six-year-old son's tee ball game and left that for a big-league version, heading to Chase Field.

With the game delayed nearly two hours, the Diamondbacks' events staff got into the mood, playing Bonnie Tyler's "Holding Out for a Hero" and other similarly themed songs through the stadium speakers as Hilton rode a scissors lift up to the swarm, covered in a protective suit and equipment, including "a non-pesticidal solution" to tranquilize the bees and a vacuum to collect them.

Dubbed "The Bee Guy," Hilton became an instant celebrity. The Diamondbacks had him stick around and throw out the ceremonial first pitch when the game finally started. He appeared on morning TV shows around the country. Topps released a trading card of "The Bee Guy," and the National Bobblehead Hall of Fame and Museum created a limited edition bobblehead of the pest control hero.

The Dodgers supplied their own sting, taking three out of four in Arizona, finishing the series with an 8–0 win as Ohtani got his first day off of the season. As the Dodgers kept a seven-game winning streak going with back-to-back three-game sweeps of the Braves and Marlins, Ohtani got hot again, hitting four home runs in a three-game span.

In a 5–1 win on May 5 that completed the sweep of the Braves, Ohtani had four hits, including two home runs. One of the homers traveled an estimated 464 feet deep into the pavilion seating at Dodger Stadium.

"He just keeps doing things that we haven't seen before," Roberts said. "That's deep. People don't hit the ball out there."

Roberts would have to repeat that multiple times over the course of the season.

"I just feel like we're overall playing really well, so that's really helping me have quality at-bats and just feeling good overall," Ohtani said of his hot streak and the team's winning streak.

When Ohtani homered on May 6 against the Marlins, he was batting .370 with 26 extra-base hits (14 doubles, one triple, 11 home runs). According to MLB.com statistician Sarah Langs, Ohtani was the first Dodger to have a .370 average and at least 25 extra-base hits in his team's first 37 games in the expansion era (since 1961).

That was enough to make him the National League Player of the Week for the opening week in May, the first such honor with his new team.

The Dodgers' hot streak began to cool off with a visit to San Diego that began on May 10. The Dodgers lost two of three to the Padres, scoring just one run total in the two losses. Ohtani came out of the game early on May 11 and was not in the lineup the next day due to lower back tightness.

"I just felt some discomfort while working out [before the game] yesterday," Ohtani said of sitting out a game. "I personally feel that I can play, but just taking it easy."

Ohtani was back in the lineup when the Dodgers traveled to San Francisco for a three-game series against the rival Giants. And he was quickly back to hammering baseballs.

In the second game, he led off the fourth inning against Giants rookie right-hander Keaton Winn and sent a breaking ball 446 feet onto the walkway behind the small seating area in right-center field.

"That's Barry territory," said Dave Roberts, a teammate of Barry Bonds for two seasons in San Francisco.

Bonds was actually in attendance that night. Ohtani expressed disappointment that he hadn't matched Bonds with a "splash hit"—a home run hit into the waters of McCovey Cove beyond right field at Oracle Park.

"I thought I hit one today," said Ohtani, who will get plenty more opportunities with the Dodgers visiting frequently over the next 10 seasons.

Fueling the best start of his career, Roberts said, was Ohtani's pleasure playing for a championship contender after six seasons of mediocrity in Anaheim.

"I think that the overarching thing that he's craved and desired for so long is to play for a winner and play for a team that's trying to play for a championship," the Dodgers manager said. "And not to take anything away from the Angels, but I think what we've done, he's seen that and I think that's raising his level of play, keeping his focus every at-bat, every day, and then you're seeing what he's capable of."

With that added focus came a greater attention to detail, making Ohtani a "considerably" better hitter in 2024 than he had been previously, Roberts said. At that point, Ohtani led the majors with a .364 average.

"I think he's always been a slugger, always will be," he said. "He's aggressive, always will be. But I think he's becoming a better hitter."

Ohtani hesitated to agree, though he did say "being in a lineup with a lot of good hitters, putting up a lot of good, quality at-bats, I think has some effect."

From all appearances, the scandal surrounding his former interpreter, Ippei Mizuhara, did not affect Ohtani's performance.

"Initially, I really didn't have much sleep, obviously, with the things that were happening," Ohtani said when the topic was raised. "But now I've been able to really have a pretty consistent routine, being able to sleep well. I think those are leading to good results."

The importance of sleep in Ohtani's routine was not surprising. It was surprising to hear Ohtani acknowledge the way Mizuhara had shaken him.

"I think really as the incidents progressed and I was able to do what I can to show that—basically doing what I can to show that I'm fine," Ohtani said in San Francisco. "As the incidents were progressing and the investigation was going on, as I was starting to not be involved anymore, that's when I was able to really focus on my sleep and being able to sleep better."

The Dodgers returned home from San Francisco for one of the biggest weeks of the season for Shohei Ohtani.

It started with his first bobblehead night as a Dodger, on May 16, and created a frenzy among Dodgers fans. A sold-out crowd of 53,527 showed up—the largest crowd at Dodger Stadium since September 2019—and they showed up early, lining the streets outside the entrances to the parking lot and snarling traffic in the area, all to make sure they got in early enough to get one of the prized promotions.

"Shohei creates a stir," Dave Roberts said.

Ticket prices spiked for the game—the first of four Ohtani-themed promotional giveaways, including two bobbleheads—and the bobbleheads quickly showed up on eBay, selling for $150 and up. Seventeen hundred versions of the bobblehead featuring Ohtani in a grey road jersey were mixed in to the giveaway. Those were listed the next day for $2,300 on eBay.

The morning after his bobblehead night (and a 7–2 loss to the Cincinnati Reds), Ohtani received another honor, as the Los Angeles City Council declared May 17 "Shohei Ohtani Day" in the city. Ohtani accepted the honor at city hall with Dave Roberts and members of the Dodgers' front office on hand to celebrate with him.

Ohtani's six years down the road in Anaheim seemed to be washed away in the excitement and newness of his emergence as a Dodger.

"It's certainly the Dodgers' fan base at the heart," Roberts said of Ohtani's popularity finding a new level in 2024. "But I think that he's somewhat of a pop culture kind of—I don't know if it's icon yet. But he's pop culture, where people just want to be in the party and be around him. That's very unique, certainly with baseball. You have it with Michael Jordan and some football players potentially. But I haven't seen anything like this yet."

Several council members took turns making statements about Ohtani Day. John Lee, a council member of Korean American heritage, praised Ohtani for giving Asian fans someone to whom they can relate.

"As someone growing up in the city who loves sports, wanting to see Asian players, wanting to see someone who looks like me, and now to have the best player in baseball not only look like someone like me but playing for the Dodgers, it's such a privilege," Lee said. "We have people in politics, we have people in entertainment...and now we have someone in sports."

Declaring days to honor sports heroes is a tried-and-true tactic among politicians, designed to create photo ops with those heroes and stir positive feelings. But the L.A. City Council took it a step further, declaring every May 17 "Shohei Ohtani Day" for as long as Ohtani plays for the Dodgers.

That prompted a pregame conversation among myself and several members of the Japanese media about what holiday traditions might be appropriate for future Ohtani Days. Should we decorate our houses like Halloween? Shoot off fireworks like the Fourth of July? Exchange gifts like Christmas?

Ohtani's locker was just a few steps away, so I went over and asked his hopes for future Ohtani Day traditions. He laughed off suggestions of gift exchanges or any themed decorations.

When I asked if there was a certain food we should eat on his day, he said, "Sushi," then turned to walk away. Over his shoulder, he added, "Or pizza."

That night, Ohtani established his own Shohei Ohtani Day tradition by hitting a home run in a 7–3 Dodgers victory over the Reds.

"He didn't homer on his bobblehead day so he was due to homer on some significant Ohtani day," Roberts joked after game. "We'll take the home run on Shohei Ohtani Day."

Ohtani reached the first Shohei Ohtani Day leading the major leagues in batting average (.360), slugging percentage (.669), OPS (1.099), and hits (63), and was tied for the MLB lead in home runs. He was the only player in either league with double-digit totals in home runs *and* stolen bases—a foreshadowing of the historic 50-50 season under construction.

The special week ended with a special moment. Ohtani drove in the game-winning run with an RBI single in the 10th inning on May 19, his first walkoff hit with the Dodgers.

"I was just looking to put the ball in play," Ohtani said. "I'm glad it worked out well."

After a rough start in clutch situations—just one hit in his first 19 at-bats with runners in scoring position—perhaps fueled by pressing to make a good first impression with his new team, Ohtani had "gotten better," Dave Roberts said.

"I think that there's certain times I think that you can expand [the strike zone]. You should expand," Roberts said after the walkoff hit. "But I think, by and large, you need to stay disciplined in your strike zone, and certainly Shohei covers more [pitches] than most players. But the last four weeks, he's been very stubborn in his strike zone, earning good pitches to hit, and when they make mistakes, he takes advantage."

Hidden away in the weekend series, though, was a play that would impact Ohtani for the next few weeks. He drew a walk in the first inning of the first game against the Reds and was hit in the back of the right leg as he dove back to first base on a pickoff attempt by Reds lefty Brent Suter.

Ohtani stole second base pitches later and didn't miss any playing time. But he suffered a contusion to his right hamstring which limited him for a few weeks.

"Our advice to him is, just be smart with it," Roberts said of letting Ohtani play through the injury. "We need him in there. So we don't want him to push it."

It did seem to affect his swing, though. In 21 games starting with the night he was hit by Suter, Ohtani was 17-for-85 (.200) with 23 strikeouts and diminished power.

"Obviously, the leg isn't that great," Ohtani admitted. "But I don't personally think it's affecting the swing. I've been working and making sure that's in a good place."

Dave Roberts said he took Ohtani at his word. But Roberts couldn't help but notice the dip in Ohtani's production in late May.

"I guess maybe he's a finely tuned machine and sometimes, in the context of a sports car, when it's not firing on all cylinders, it just doesn't run right," Roberts said.

The same metaphor soon applied to the Dodgers.

Injuries were a part of the picture even before the season started.

Veteran left-hander Clayton Kershaw underwent shoulder surgery in November 2023, the first surgery of his Hall of Fame career, and was not expected back until midseason.

Reliever Brusdar Graterol had shoulder pain in spring training and would not make his season debut until August.

Veteran Blake Treinen was hit in the ribs by a line drive during one of the last Cactus League exhibition games and, combined with his shoulder surgery in 2022, didn't make his return until May. Rookie right-hander Emmet Sheehan was expected to compete for a spot in the 2024 starting rotation but an elbow injury led to Tommy John surgery that sidelined him until 2025. He joined fellow starters Dustin May and Tony Gonsolin, also recovering from elbow surgeries in 2023 and not expected back until the 2025 season.

The Dodgers thought they had addressed the need for starting pitching depth with the off-season acquisitions of Tyler Glasnow, Yoshinobu Yamamoto, and James Paxton. But Glasnow would make two trips to the Injured List during the 2024 season, and Yamamoto spent nearly three months on the IL with a rotator cuff strain. Paxton, meanwhile, was deemed expendable after an unimpressive first-half performance and was traded to the Boston Red Sox in July. Shortly after, his season was ended by a calf injury.

At the All-Star break, the Dodgers had an MLB-leading 15 players on the Injured List, with the pitching staff hardest hit. Seventeen different pitchers started at least one game for the Dodgers in 2024. Eleven of them spent time on the Injured List.

"It's been a really challenging year on that front and something that we're going to need to spend a lot of time on this winter to really dig in on," Andrew Friedman said in September. "From when we onboard a pitcher—when we draft or trade for him—through the development path, at the major-league level, obviously it's a problem in the industry, and the injuries that are happening to us, we feel. Injuries that are happening to other teams, we don't feel as much. It doesn't hit home quite the same way. And so we're going to do everything we can to put ourselves in the best position going forward."

Under Friedman, the Dodgers have been unafraid to "onboard" players with extensive injury histories, both via the draft and at the major-league level—like selecting Walker Buehler in the first round of the 2015 draft, even though he was about to undergo Tommy John surgery, or trading for Glasnow in December 2023, knowing he had stayed healthy enough to pitch more than 100 innings just twice in his first eight big-league seasons.

But the Dodgers have also been among the most proactive in trying to protect their pitchers. Motivated in part by Glasnow's history and Yamamoto's lack of experience with a major-league schedule, the Dodgers' starting pitcher had at least five days' rest before taking the mound 144 times in 162 regular-season games.

"I can't imagine there's a team that has their guys go on extra rest more than us," Friedman said. "Looking at bullpen usage, we're near the more conservative, near the top in terms of being conservative. That's not helping in terms of staving off injuries."

They were not alone. The frequency of pitcher injuries has climbed in recent seasons, so much so that three-time Cy Young Award winner Justin Verlander called it "a pandemic" in 2024—as he was on a rehab assignment recovering from a shoulder injury.

"I really don't have any solutions to it," Buehler said on the *Just Baseball* podcast, himself returning in 2024 from a second Tommy John surgery. "I could go on and on about the pros and cons of everything. But it just kind of sucks."

Myriad factors have been cited as causes—everything from the increase in velocity and focus on spin rate to the crackdown on "sticky stuff" used by pitchers and the implementation of a pitch clock in its second season at the major-league level. The players' union released a statement early in the 2024 season, pointing to MLB's unilateral decision to shave two seconds off the pitch clock this season.

"I'm sure there's some added pressure just to the body in having to maintain a workload in less amount of time," Ohtani said of the pitch clock. "So just personally, I'm sure there could be [a connection]. But nothing concrete to be able to say that is the sole reason why."

The Dodgers traveled to Pittsburgh in early June to face two examples of the new age of high-velocity pitchers—hard-throwing right-handers Jared Jones and eventual NL Rookie of the Year Paul Skenes.

Jones held the Dodgers to three hits over six scoreless innings in a 1–0 Pirates win to open the series. Skenes started the second game and struck out Ohtani in the first inning, challenging him with three straight fastballs. The final one whizzed past Ohtani at 101 mph.

Two innings later, the two squared off for the second time. Skenes challenged Ohtani again but this time Ohtani turned on a full-count, 100-mph fastball and sent it 415 feet out to center field for a two-run home run.

The Dodgers would go on to lose. But the Skenes-Ohtani matchup was a highlight of the series.

"I like to call that 'big on big,'" Skenes said of challenging Ohtani with his fastball. "I obviously beat him a couple times earlier [in the first inning]. I think that was the right pitch to throw there [in the second at-bat].... Gotta kind of tip your cap. He's a good player and stuff like that is going to happen."

An Orange County native, the 22-year-old Skenes grew up going to Angels games and said he was there with his El Toro High School baseball teammates for Ohtani's first home start as a pitcher for the Angels.

Ohtani said he was "not really surprised" Skenes challenged him with his fastball.

"His stuff itself was really good. As you saw in my first at-bat, I couldn't really put together good swings," Ohtani said. "Rather than the velo[city], it's really the angle [of Skenes' delivery] and the release. So I made the adjustment the second at-bat."

Ohtani had just two hits in 14 at-bats before the home run off Skenes. But he added a single later in the game that left his bat at 107.6 mph. It was his first multi-hit game in a week and Dave Roberts took it as a positive sign that Ohtani might be over the bruised hamstring that had sent him into a brief slump.

"You can tell he's been taking some extra swings, trying to work through some things," Roberts said in Pittsburgh. "To see him hit a homer to center field, to be on time for velocity, to take some borderline pitches—he's obviously one of the best hitters in the game, so to get him back in the [strike] zone and hitting the ball hard like he did tonight is certainly a good sign."

Ohtani's downturn wasn't over yet, though. The Dodgers went from Pittsburgh to New York for a three-game series at Yankee Stadium featuring the two MVP favorites, Yankees slugger Aaron Judge and Ohtani, and a playoff atmosphere—in the stands and with the media turnout.

The Dodgers rose to the moment and took two out of three from the Yankees. Yoshinobu Yamamoto set the tone in the first game, holding the Yankees to two hits while striking out seven in seven scoreless innings. Ohtani was just 2-for-13 in the series.

Ohtani briefly appeared to be back in the swing of things after the Dodgers returned home to face the Texas Rangers, hitting home runs in each of the first two games of the series. But the man of the hour was Rangers veteran reliever David Robertson.

The 39-year-old right-hander was in the 16th season of a big-league career that saw him pitch out of the bullpen for eight different teams. On June 12 at Dodger Stadium, Rangers manager Bruce Bochy called on Robertson to protect a 3–1 lead in the eighth inning. The top of the Dodgers' order—Mookie Betts, Shohei Ohtani, and Freddie Freeman—was set to bat.

"Before this series, the only time I got him out was in spring training as a Brave," Robertson said later of the matchup with Freeman, in particular.

The Dodgers first baseman was 4-for-4 in his career against the well-traveled Robertson up to that point. Betts was 4-for-11.

"When they got me up [in the bullpen], I told [Rangers closer Kirby Yates], 'I don't think somebody has looked at the numbers,'" Robertson joked later.

Robertson struck out the trio of former MVPs. The Dodgers scored a run in the ninth off Yates but lost, 3–2.

One night later, the scenario repeated itself. Again, Bochy called on Robertson to protect a 3–1 lead in the eighth inning. Robertson hit Cavan Biggio with a pitch and gave up a single to

Austin Barnes, putting the tying runs on base—and bringing up the top of the Dodgers' order.

But Robertson did it again, striking out Betts, Ohtani, and Freeman to preserve the lead as the Rangers went on to win again.

"It's fun when it's over," Robertson said of matching up against the Dodgers' dangerous trio.

Robertson had never faced Ohtani before. But he struck him out with the same pitch sequence each night—cutter, cutter, knuckle curve.

"There was really nothing surprising as the data lays him out," Ohtani said. "He's just been able to execute the pitches and get outs."

Despite the two home runs against the Rangers, Ohtani's slump had continued. In the 24 games after being hit in the leg by Brent Suter's pickoff throw, Ohtani had hit just .200 (19-for-95). Not coincidentally, the Dodgers were a .500 team (12–12) during that stretch.

"There's always going to be stretches of ups and downs—as a team and personally," Ohtani said. "Obviously when things aren't going well, that's when we put everything under a microscope. My approach has been the same, just trying to put up quality at-bats."

Things were about to change.

Chapter 6

The Injured List

For the first six weeks or so of the 2024 season, the Dodgers' injury issues were largely confined to the pitching staff. The core of their lineup—Mookie Betts, Shohei Ohtani, and Freddie Freeman at the top; Teoscar Hernández, Will Smith, and Max Muncy in the middle—was healthy.

Then Muncy felt something grab on his right side while taking batting practice before the game against the Cincinnati Reds on May 16. Muncy was not scheduled to play that night. When he was examined by the team's medical staff and underwent a scan, the diagnosis was a mild strain of an oblique muscle in his right side. The emphasis was on "mild." Dodgers manager Dave Roberts said, at first, the team wasn't even sure a trip to the Injured List was necessary.

Out of caution, the Dodgers put Muncy on the IL with the expectation that he would be ready to play again after the minimum 10 days on the sidelines.

"I think we got ahead of it," Roberts said at the time. "Certainly [he's going on the] IL, as far as kind of giving him a handful of days to recover. I'm sure he's not going to swing the bat for a couple, two, three days, and the hope is he'll be back online on the 11th day."

Muncy didn't play again until August 19.

Over a frustrating three months, Muncy did what activity he could. But every time he tried to increase the activity or start swinging a bat, the discomfort would return.

"I'd have a good day and then I'd wake up and it'd feel like Day One of the injury," Muncy said later.

By mid-June, with no progress in his recovery, Muncy called it "terrible" and sitting out so long "one of the hardest things that I've had to do."

Multiple times, he tried increasing his activity, hitting off a tee or swinging against soft tosses from a coach, only to have to shut it down.

"I've had injuries in the past but nothing that's kept me out for this long," he said. "It's been a tough one for me. It's been a very frustrating one for me."

It wasn't until late July that Muncy's mystery was solved. He underwent multiple examinations while sitting out. Finally, one of those exams revealed that one of his bottom ribs was "out of place." A "chiropractic adjustment" put the rib back in place and Muncy's pain dissipated, allowing him to progress in a rehab program and finally return to the lineup with two home runs, two doubles, and six RBI in a late August sweep of the Seattle Mariners.

The Dodgers were averaging 5.3 runs per game before Muncy's injury. That dropped to just 4.7 runs per game in the first 35 games he missed. The Dodgers' collection of replacements—primarily veteran utilityman Kiké Hernández and Cavan Biggio (obtained from the Toronto Blue Jays)—combined to hit just .168 with only five extra-base hits (three doubles and two home runs).

The bottom half of the Dodgers' lineup had been fairly unproductive in the opening weeks of the season. It became a serious drag on the offense after Muncy left.

"It lacks potential slug," Roberts said of the depleted lineup. "It lacks a guy who's going to get on base 38 percent of the time. It lacks just the consistency of the left-right to kind of vary it whether it's [versus] the starter or bullpen. Just that continuity, one through six.

"Instead, we've been piece-mealing the five, six [spots in the lineup] and trying to beat the starter. Where you just know that having a guy like Max in there—versus left[-handed pitchers], versus right—when he's in there they have to approach our lineup differently."

Significant as Muncy's absence was, bigger blows were coming.

The Dodgers went to New York for a star-studded series at Yankee Stadium. The Dodgers and Yankees—perhaps the sport's most storied franchises—had two of the three best records in baseball at the time (the Philadelphia Phillies were also at the top) and former MVPs forging new MVP campaigns—Aaron Judge with the Yankees, Shohei Ohtani with the Dodgers.

The combination intensified the coverage by the media and heightened the intensity from the crowds.

"It felt like a playoff game today," Teoscar Hernández said after the series opener.

Yoshinobu Yamamoto was up to the moment. He held the Yankees scoreless for seven innings, allowing just two hits while striking out seven. The game stayed scoreless until the 11th inning with the Dodgers ultimately winning, 2–1.

But Yamamoto's big-game performance was the story of the day.

"His best outing as a Dodger," Roberts said that night. "You could just see it. He felt it. He knew we needed it. And it brought out the best in him. I can't say enough about his effort tonight."

The Dodgers took two of three in the series. But Yamamoto's effort would prove costly.

The Dodgers pushed his next start back, giving him a full week off before he took the mound again, against the Kansas City Royals at Dodger Stadium. He stayed for just two innings before leaving with shoulder pain.

Was the injury a result of Yamamoto pushing himself too far in Yankee Stadium? Was it because he added the slider back in as a prominent part of his pitch mix? In any case, he was diagnosed with a strained rotator cuff, an injury that sidelined him for almost three months. It was one of the biggest blows to a Dodgers' starting rotation that was depleted enough to prompt the front office to make it a priority at the July trade deadline. Jack Flaherty was acquired from the Detroit Tigers to help address the problem.

But the biggest loss came a day later.

The Dodgers were leading the Royals 3–0 on a pair of home runs from Ohtani (his 18th and 19th of the season) and one from Freddie Freeman when Mookie Betts came to bat in the seventh inning against Royals reliever Dan Altavilla.

Altavilla came inside with a 1-and-2 fastball. The 98-mph pitch caught Betts flush on the back of his left hand. Betts dropped to the ground immediately, rolling around in pain. The news came quickly after the game—Betts had suffered a fractured left hand and would miss four to six weeks.

"I just went numb and it hurt," Betts said after the game. "You just gotta stay in there. Can't be scared, you know, kind of stay there, especially with a guy with a pretty good slider. Just kind of up and in. I was holding my ground. Unfortunately it hit me in the hand."

Betts had cooled off from his hot start but was still hitting .304 with an .892 OPS at the time of the injury, while handling shortstop on an everyday basis for the Dodgers.

"It's a big blow. It is," Roberts said. "I feel really bad for Mookie. He was obviously having an MVP-type season."

Betts, in fact, might have been the only real threat to Ohtani winning his third MVP. But he wouldn't play for five weeks while his hand healed.

"Very tough to see as a teammate," Ohtani said. "He's obviously a very important part of the team. If he's out for some time, it's really up to the rest of the team to pick him up."

Most of that burden, however, would fall on Ohtani himself.

With Betts out of the lineup, Roberts moved Ohtani into the leadoff spot. Ohtani made himself comfortable there quickly. He had three hits and scored two runs in a win over the Colorado Rockies the day after Betts went down.

"It was by default," Roberts said of the decision to move Ohtani into the leadoff spot. "We had no one else. So he's a perfect default. He's done it before. And honestly, he's swinging the bat well there and he was starting to swing the bat better before that."

Ohtani had indeed batted leadoff before—but not that often. He made 61 starts as the leadoff hitter in six seasons with the Angels, most of those in 2021 (23) and 2022 (32), spending much more time in the second or third spots.

Ohtani had been slumping before the move. In 19 games before the two-homer game against the Royals on June 16, Ohtani had hit just .195 with 22 strikeouts in 77 at-bats. In his first 13 games as the Dodgers' leadoff man, he was 19-for-50 (.380) with eight home runs, 18 RBIs, and 16 runs scored.

"I mean, it doesn't matter where that guy hits, he's going to hit," Freddie Freeman said.

During the series in Colorado, Ohtani hit a 476-foot home run off left-hander Austin Gomber. At the time, it was the longest home run of the season—and the longest home run of Ohtani's career.

"All the time," Dodgers pitcher Tyler Glasnow said when asked if Ohtani's teammates are ever amazed by Ohtani's feats. "I feel like everybody's reaction is always, like, 'Wow!' Like, every time. I think we're all still—it's very entertaining for all of us as well."

After failing to sign Shohei Ohtani in 2017, Dodgers owner Mark Walter (left) and president Andrew Friedman (right) finally got their man in 2023. The team signed Ohtani to a 10-year, $700 million deal, at the time the largest contract in sports history. (AP Photo/Ashley Landis)

The team also signed Ohtani's fellow countryman Yoshinobu Yamamoto, part of a holiday spending spree that saw the Dodgers commit more than a billion dollars in salaries. (AP Photo/Ashley Landis)

Ohtani was followed by scores of media members everywhere he went, including a large contingent from his native Japan. (AP Photo/Richard Vogel)

Ohtani, the Dodgers, and the world of baseball were rocked by the revelation in March 2024 that his longtime translator, Ippei Mizuhara (left), had stolen millions of dollars from Ohtani to cover his own gambling debts. (AP Photo/Richard Vogel)

Mookie Betts (left), Freddie Freeman (middle), and Ohtani gave the Dodgers three former league MVPs at the top of their lineup. (Nick Wosika/Icon Sportswire via AP Images)

The frenzy and attention around Ohtani extended to his dog, Decoy, who "threw" out the first pitch before a Dodgers home game in August. (AP Photo/Mark J. Terrill)

In his first All-Star Game appearance as a National Leaguer, Ohtani homered off Boston right-hander Tanner Houck in the third inning. He became the first player in All-Star history to both win the game—he was the starting pitcher and won in 2021—and to hit a home run in one. (Kyodo via AP Images)

Ohtani clinched the first 50-50 season in baseball history in dramatic fashion; his steal of third in the first inning (above) against the Miami Marlins and his home run in the seventh (below) were part of a 6-for-6, three-homer, 10-RBI performance. (AP Photo/Wilfredo Lee; AP Photo/Marta Lavandier)

Though Ohtani rehabbed from his 2023 elbow surgery throughout the 2024 season, the Dodgers never seriously considered allowing him to return to the mound for the postseason. (AP Photo/Gregory Bull)

His return to the mound in 2025 would be further delayed after Ohtani suffered a torn labrum during Game 2 of the World Series against the New York Yankees. (The Yomiuri Shimbun via AP Images)

With Ohtani limited by injury, his Dodgers teammates stepped up at the plate and on the mound. Freeman's walkoff grand slam in Game 1 (above) was the first in World Series history, and starting pitcher Walter Buehler came out of the bullpen to save Game 5 (below) for Los Angeles' first full-season championship since 1988. (AP Photo/Ashley Landis; AP Photo/Frank Franklin II)

Faced with weighty expectations, plenty of off-field distractions, and numerous injuries to key players, Dodgers manager Dave Roberts guided Ohtani and his team to the franchise's seventh World Series championship since moving to L.A. (AP Photo/Julio Cortez)

One of the biggest roars at the championship rally came when Ohtani took the microphone and addressed the crowd in English. "This is such a special moment for me," he said. "I'm so honored to be here and to be part of this team. Congratulations, Los Angeles. Thank you, fans." (AP Photo/Mark J. Terrill)

But the highlight of that June 18 game came in the ninth inning. Trailing 9–4 in the ninth inning, the Dodgers exploded for seven runs, including a pinch-hit grand slam by Jason Heyward and a go-ahead three-run home run by Teoscar Hernández to cap an amazing comeback at Coors Field.

Ohtani was named the National League's Player of the Week after his first week in the leadoff spot. He went 11-for-24 (.458) with four home runs, 11 RBIs, three doubles, a 1.083 slugging percentage, and a .567 on-base percentage in six games—including two against his former team, the Angels.

"Just pure talent. Shohei is on a different level," Roberts said of the hot streak. "But now you layer in the plate discipline and that puts him on another level. I believe talent can get you a long way. But to be disciplined in the strike zone makes you even more dangerous—willing to take first base via the walk, willing to take a 3-2 slider that's a ball. Those things are separators, and that's what he's doing."

Ohtani insisted "nothing really meaningful changed" with his move into the leadoff spot. But he agreed with Roberts that having "really good awareness of the strike zone" had led to his latest hot streak.

He homered in each of the two games against the Angels at Dodger Stadium (each team winning once) but dismissed the matchup against his old teammates as nothing special, since it was a home game for the Dodgers.

"I'm sure it's going to feel a little different when we play at Angel Stadium," he said.

The biggest difference for Ohtani, though, was playing for a championship contender after six seasons of mediocrity—or worse—in Anaheim. He acknowledged he was enjoying things more in Los Angeles.

"Yes—and I'm sure more so as we head into the second half of the season," he said through his interpreter after the June 21 game against the Angels. "It's something I really haven't experienced in the past, so I'm looking forward to that."

Ohtani's surge in the leadoff spot continued during a three-game sweep of the historically awful Chicago White Sox. He hit two more home runs, giving him eight in his past 10 games, five in his past six, and a National League–leading 25 for the season. From June 16 against the Royals through June 22 against the Angels, Ohtani had an RBI, an extra-base hit, and scored a run in seven consecutive games. The RBI streak extended to 10 consecutive games, the longest by a Dodger since RBIs became an official stat, in 1920.

"There have been a lot of opportunities with runners on base," Ohtani said. "All I'm trying to do is have a quality at-bat. So I think it [the RBI streak] is a result of that."

He had home runs during his latest hot streak that covered 476 and 459 feet (in Colorado), and 455 and 451 feet (at Dodger Stadium). Since Statcast began tracking everything in 2015, no player had hit two 450-foot home runs at Dodger Stadium. Ohtani did it in back-to-back games.

Ohtani's power display raised the possibility that he would participate in the Home Run Derby during the All-Star festivities at Globe Life Field in Arlington, Texas.

"I'm rehabbing [from his 2023 elbow surgery] so I would need to get clearance from the doctor, the trainers, and the team," Ohtani said when asked about the possibility. "Of course, there's a feeling that I want to participate. I think any player feels the same way. So it depends on all the other factors."

Those other factors proved decisive. Ohtani has participated in the Home Run Derby just once—in 2021, at Coors Field in Denver, where he hit six home runs of 500 feet or longer. Ultimately, Ohtani would pass on doing it in Texas, citing his elbow rehab as the reason. Instead, his teammate and good friend, Teoscar Hernández, became the first Dodgers player to win the Home Run Derby, beating the Royals' young shortstop Bobby Witt Jr. in a close final.

Dave Roberts applauded Ohtani for his priorities.

"He signed up here to help us win a championship and nothing should get in the way of that," he said. "In any other normal situation where he wasn't rehabbing, I think he would love to participate. I know that it's weighed heavy on him. But I do think the rehab process is something that ultimately makes him feel better about bowing out. It's just not his responsibility alone to carry the game of baseball. He does it on a daily basis."

During the Dodgers' late-June series in Chicago, it was nearly Shohei Ohtani's turn to go down with an injury—but Javier Herrera earned possibly the biggest save of the Dodgers' season.

The 38-year-old member of the team's clubhouse staff was standing on the top step of the Dodgers' dugout during the third inning. With Kiké Hernández at bat, Shohei Ohtani was two hitters away and was preparing by the bat rack in the dugout when Hernández fouled a ball off.

The ball shot toward the Dodgers' dugout where Herrera nonchalantly reached out and caught it as it seemed to be heading for a distracted Ohtani. The save was caught on the TV broadcast and the video quickly went viral.

"I was just doing my job," Herrera said when the media surrounded him before the Dodgers' next game. "I saw the pitch all the way through, hit the bat, and the ball pretty much found me."

A member of the Dodgers' staff for 18 years, Herrera blushed at all the attention when the media sought him out. Ohtani posted a photo of the scene on Instagram with the words "My Hero!" overlaid on the photo.

"Someone sent me the video and I saw it 100 times," Herrera said. "It was pretty impressive. I was impressed. But in the moment, it was just like, 'Okay, let's keep playing.'"

It wasn't Herrera's first brush with celebrity after a foul ball. During a game at Dodger Stadium in August 2016, he was serving as the ball boy down the left-field line and tumbled head first over the wall and into the stands while trying to catch a foul ball. That video made the rounds as well.

This attention was much better, Herrera agreed.

"Yeah, definitely," he said. "I fell on my—I fell. I fell [the other time] and I'm the hero on this one, I guess. The other one, I was more of a joke. It was more embarrassing."

Ohtani's surge in the leadoff spot continued with a three-hit game (including his 27th home run of the season) on July 2, against the Arizona Diamondbacks—a night that drew 52,931 fans to Dodger Stadium to celebrate Japanese Heritage Night and ended with a walkoff win for the Dodgers.

"Shohei is very storybook," Roberts said of giving the fans what they came to see. "It seems like whenever there's anticipation for something to happen, it happens. And guys like that are like Michael Jordan or Tiger Woods. Just look back at the WBC [World Baseball Classic in 2023]—him versus [Mike] Trout, that one where he was pitching. And then on Japanese Heritage Night, obviously you've got so many people from Japan here. And then he comes up huge."

The Dodgers won nine of the first 13 games following Betts' injury and sat comfortably atop the National League West division, 8½ games ahead of the second-place San Diego Padres. Only the Philadelphia Phillies had a better record in the National League to that point.

But things turned less positive as the Dodgers celebrated the Fourth of July holiday at home with a 9–3 loss to the Diamondbacks. Ohtani walked in his first appearance then struck out in each of his next three at-bats.

That ended Ohtani's 20s. He turned 30 on July 5 as the Dodgers beat the Milwaukee Brewers, 8–5. But Ohtani went hitless and struck out in his first three at-bats, making it a career-high six consecutive at-bats that ended in strikeouts.

Ohtani was chasing pitches—particularly breaking pitches—below the strike zone, Dave Roberts said, expressing confidence that Ohtani would "reset."

"It's easy [to believe that] because he's had stretches of a couple, two, three, four games where he does that and then he resets and gets back in the zone," Roberts said.

All was well a day later. Ohtani reached base five times on two walks, a hit by pitch, a triple, and a 430-foot home run in another win over the Brewers. But all the injuries were beginning to take their toll on the team.

After losing the series finale to the Brewers, the Dodgers headed on the road for the final week before the All-Star break, starting in Philadelphia with a matchup between the teams with the two best records in the National League.

It didn't go well. The Phillies had their way against the Dodgers' depleted pitching staff. They swept the Dodgers in the three-game series at Citizens Bank Park, outscoring them 19–5 and leading at the end of all but one inning during the three games. It was the first time the Dodgers had been swept in Philadelphia since May 2004.

"We didn't play very good that series," Freeman said after the third loss. "We didn't hit. We didn't do much. As a group, we just have to put it behind us, go to Detroit tomorrow, and try to win a series."

Things didn't get better in Detroit.

Tyler Glasnow's lower back pain landed him on the Injured List, joining fellow starters Yoshinobu Yamamoto (rotator cuff), Clayton Kershaw (shoulder), and Walker Buehler (hip). Glasnow would return to pitch just 25 innings after the All-Star break before an elbow injury ended his season.

With few options among their starting pitchers, the Dodgers starters for the three-game series in Detroit were veteran James Paxton, rookie Justin Wrobleski (in his second big-league start), and Brent Honeywell Jr., who was claimed off waivers from the Pittsburgh Pirates on Saturday and started for the Dodgers in Detroit on Sunday.

"If you're talking about the last game before the All-Star break, in a day game on the road, and it's a waiver claim—it's desperate times, absolutely," Roberts admitted.

At the same time, the lineup was still missing Mookie Betts and Max Muncy.

"I mean, we are injured. We have a lot of guys missing," Freeman said. "No one really cares about that. Nor does anyone in here. [However] we are missing a top-five player in the game of baseball in Mookie. Our rotation has taken a hit."

But it wasn't the starters that let them down in Detroit. After winning the first game of the series at Comerica Park on Ohtani's ninth-inning RBI double, the Dodgers' overworked bullpen collapsed in the next two games. They blew a five-run lead in the ninth inning on July 13, then lost in 10 innings. On July 14, it was a one-run lead that got away as the Tigers walked them off for the second consecutive game after Dodgers reliever Yohan Ramírez misplayed two consecutive bunts.

The Dodgers reached the All-Star break in first place in the NL West for the eighth time in the past 10 full seasons. But they were staggering, with just one win in their final seven games and just five in their last 15.

Moreover, they had largely muddled along as a .500 team for most of the first half. They were just 26–24 in the 50 games before the All-Star break, 15–15 since the end of that exciting series at Yankee Stadium, and—not surprising—just 12–12 since losing Mookie Betts to injury.

"It's been difficult," Roberts said. "I said this a few days ago—it feels like we have to play perfect baseball. And that's not the way it should be for us to win baseball games. But where we're at—it's hard putting runs across and you feel like the starting pitchers, the relievers, they have to be perfect. And that's just hard to do."

For Shohei Ohtani, though, it was an overwhelmingly successful first half in his debut season with the Dodgers. He reached the All-Star break batting .316 with 29 home runs, 69 RBIs, and a 1.036 OPS. He became only the second player in National League history to reach the break with at least 50 extra-base hits (Ohtani had 23 doubles and four triples to go with his 29 home runs) and 20 or more stolen bases (he had 23). Bobby Bonds did it with the San Francisco Giants in 1973.

"Shohei has been great," Roberts said of Ohtani's first half. "He has bought into what we do as an organization, what we do as an offense. He's a great player, obviously. He's an equally great teammate. I just love obviously being able to write his name in the lineup every night. He has been fun to watch."

Ohtani headed to the All-Star Game for the fourth time in his career, starting at DH and batting second for the National League, this time at Globe Life Field in Texas. After walking in his first at-bat against Baltimore starter Corbin Burnes, Ohtani launched a three-run home run 400 feet into the right-field seats off Red Sox right-hander Tanner Houck in the third inning.

It was Ohtani's first home run in an All-Star Game and wrote his name once again in the record books. He is the only player in All-Star history to both win the game—he was the starting pitcher and won in 2021—and to hit a home run in one.

"It's Shohei being Shohei," teammate Teoscar Hernández said.

"It felt inevitable he was going to do it," said Freeman, another one of the four Dodgers who played in the game. "He steps in the box and you kind of figure he would come through. Pretty awesome."

The Dodgers' problems were still waiting for them after the All-Star break. But the rest seemed to reinvigorate them. They swept a three-game series from the Boston Red Sox and took three of four from the San Francisco Giants.

Ohtani was at the center of the first two wins against the Red Sox. His one-out double in the eighth inning of the first game helped load the bases for Freddie Freeman, whose grand slam gave the Dodgers a come-from-behind 4–1 win.

The second game went into the bottom of the 11th inning tied. With runners on first and third and one out, Red Sox manager Alex Cora chose to intentionally walk Ohtani and face Will Smith. The Dodgers catcher came through with a walkoff RBI single.

Ohtani took center stage in the third game, hitting one of the longest home runs in Dodger Stadium history during a 9–6 win that completed the sweep.

The Dodgers hit six home runs in the game, none more impressive than Ohtani's in the fifth inning. He crushed a cut fastball from Red Sox right-hander Kutter Crawford. The ball left Ohtani's bat at 116.7 mph and soared over the pavilion seats just to the right of straightaway center field. It disappeared just under the wavy roof over the pavilion seats and wound up in the walkway of the Centerfield Plaza (an area of food concessions and a gathering spot for fans).

The 30th home run of Ohtani's season traveled an estimated 473 feet and came within a few feet of leaving the stadium entirely. Only six balls have been hit out of Dodger Stadium in the facility's 62-year history; Fernando Tatís Jr., Giancarlo

Stanton, Mark McGwire, Mike Piazza, and Willie Stargell all did it by pulling the ball.

"He just never ceases to amaze," Dodgers manager Dave Roberts said of Ohtani's blast. "It's just hard to fathom someone hitting a baseball like that.... That's just where people don't go. Just really impressive. He does things—it seems like every night—that people just can't do, and I'm happy he's wearing a Dodger uniform."

Backup catcher Austin Barnes was in the dugout after hitting a home run of his own right before Ohtani when he heard what sounded "like a gunshot and everybody screaming."

"He's a freak," Barnes said. "I've never seen someone like him."

"He's superhuman, man," pitcher James Paxton said.

After the game, Ohtani admitted it is a goal to someday hit a ball out of Dodger Stadium, joining Stargell as the only left-handed hitters to do it.

"That's what I hope," he said through his interpreter. "I think I'm going to have a lot more opportunities to do so. So definitely looking forward to one of those."

According to statistician Sarah Langs, Ohtani's 473-foot drive was only the 53rd home run hit 440 feet or more at Dodger Stadium since 2015, the third-fewest of any MLB stadium (behind Oracle Park in San Francisco and Petco Park in San Diego). Ohtani had already hit six of them in 2024, the most by any player at Dodger Stadium.

It was also Ohtani's seventh home run of 450 feet or more. No other player had more than four at that point in the season.

The home run also made Ohtani only the seventh player in major-league history to hit 30 home runs and steal 20 or more bases in his team's first 100 games in a season, joining Tatís (2021), Christian Yelich (2019), José Ramírez (2018), Alfonso Soriano (2006), Jeff Bagwell (1999), and Alex Rodriguez (1998).

The 6–1 homestand ended with the return of Clayton Kershaw. Starting for the first time since shoulder surgery in November 2023, the three-time Cy Young Award winner pitched four innings and allowed two runs in the delayed start of his 17th big-league season. The game was tied in the bottom of the eighth inning when Nick Ahmed and Shohei Ohtani hit back-to-back home runs to give the Dodgers the win.

The successful homestand ended somberly, though. Dodgers first baseman Freddie Freeman traveled to Houston for the start of an eight-game road trip but quickly left the team and returned to California where his three-year-old son, Maximus, had been hospitalized.

Freeman's wife, Chelsea, had rushed Maximus to the hospital when the young boy was unable to sit up, stand, or walk for three days, and was also not eating. After some anxious days, Maximus was diagnosed with Guillain-Barré syndrome, a rare neurological disorder. It is a treatable disease from which most people completely recover.

Maximus did eventually improve and was released from the hospital, making progress in his recovery with physical therapy.

In the meantime, Freeman—who missed a total of 11 games during the previous six seasons—was out of the Dodgers' lineup for eight games. With Mookie Betts and Max Muncy still out with injuries, Shohei Ohtani was left alone at the top of the Dodgers' lineup. He went hitless for 19 consecutive plate appearances on that trip, during which the Dodgers won just three games. Over the first six games (three in Houston, two in San Diego, and the first one in Oakland), the Dodgers' lineup had 37 hits while striking out 77 times.

Ohtani admitted he hadn't been feeling "too great at the plate" during that hitless stretch—which ended with a three-run home run on August 2. But he didn't attribute that to opposing pitchers being able to pitch around him with Betts and Freeman missing from the lineup.

"It's more about myself and how I'm feeling at the plate," Ohtani said. "Balls that I'm supposed to be hitting well, I'm not. Fly balls that should have gone out haven't been going out. Line drives right at guys. It's more about me than the team or how a team is attacking me."

Nonetheless, Ohtani did manage to steal two bases against the Oakland A's on August 3, giving him 31 steals to go with his 33 home runs to that point. It was the 70th 30-30 season in MLB history but only the fourth 30-30 season by a Dodger player—Matt Kemp did it in 2011 and Raúl Mondesí did it twice, in 1997 and again in 1999.

Ohtani had matched his career-high with 26 steals in his first 100 games of the season and reached the 30-30 milestone in the Dodgers' 111th game of the season, one of the fastest 30-30 seasons in MLB history. Only Eric Davis (90 games in 1987) and Alex Rodriguez (107 games in 1998) reached the marks faster.

Kemp finished his 30-30 season just one home run short of a 40-40 season, something accomplished by only five players in major-league history at that point. At Dodger Stadium for a promotional event, Kemp was asked if Ohtani could get to 40-40.

"Oh, he's got that easy," Kemp said, laughing. "He'll beat me, because he's got 35 home runs and it's not even September."

The in-season trade deadline arrived and the Dodgers were one of the more active teams, acquiring pitcher Jack Flaherty from the Detroit Tigers, hard-throwing reliever Michael Kopech from the Chicago White Sox, utilityman Tommy Edman from the St. Louis Cardinals, and four-time Gold Glove–winning center fielder Kevin Kiermaier from the Toronto Blue Jays.

Kopech would prove a valuable addition to the bullpen, quickly settling into a crucial role in relief. Edman did not play his first game of the season until mid-August. His return from off-season wrist surgery was delayed by an ankle injury suffered during his rehab. His versatility made him a valuable piece, flipping between center field and shortstop, and, as Mookie Betts would eventually put it, filling "a void I didn't even know we had."

But none of the acquisitions was more important than Flaherty, a front-of-the-rotation starter for a rotation battered and short-handed.

"We had a ton of conversations with a lot of teams over this last week," Dodgers GM Brandon Gomes said after the deadline passed. "We felt like getting an impact starter was a very high priority for us and Jack is definitely that. His command, his stuff, the swing and miss, we feel like that's a real power option come October, so he fits into this rotation really well."

Flaherty demonstrated that immediately, pitching six scoreless innings against the A's in his first start with the Dodgers. It was the first of 10 regular-season starts he would make with the Dodgers, going 6–2 with a 3.58 ERA.

The Dodgers returned home from that trip to face the Philadelphia Phillies. Freddie Freeman rejoined the lineup, and his teammates showed their support by wearing "MaxStrong" T-shirts—they would stick around all season—and a large crowd at Dodger Stadium gave Freddie a standing ovation before his first at-bat.

"I wasn't expecting it but very much appreciated from the Dodger fans," said Freeman, who struck out in that at-bat. "They made it really hard to hit in that first at-bat. But I was okay with that. It was one of the most pleasant strikeouts I've ever had in my big-league career."

Ohtani had a double, a home run, and two RBIs in a Dodgers win that day—the only time they would beat the Phillies in six regular-season meetings.

"Being able to win with Freddie being back for the first time, that was really important for us," Ohtani said. "As a teammate, as an observer, it was very touching to be able to see that [ovation]. I'm sure his son has some rehab to do, but very much looking forward to him getting better."

The Dodgers were also looking forward to getting better. Both Max Muncy and Mookie Betts were ready to return to the lineup in mid-August. Walker Buehler and Yoshinobu Yamamoto were also at various stages of throwing programs that would get them back for the stretch run.

Chapter 7

Pitching Again

Tommy John had already put together a pretty good career as a left-handed pitcher in the big leagues when he took the mound for the Los Angeles Dodgers against the Montreal Expos on July 17, 1974.

John made the majors for a handful of games with the Cleveland Indians in 1963, and by 1974 had been a reliable, successful big-league pitcher for 12 seasons. He had won 124 games with a 2.97 ERA. Traded to the Dodgers in exchange for Dick Allen before the 1972 season, he was an outstanding addition to the Los Angeles staff. He went 40–15 with a 2.89 ERA in his first three seasons with the Dodgers.

But something happened that night at Dodger Stadium as John faced Bob Bailey, a veteran third baseman batting in the middle of the Expos' lineup, in the third inning.

"I can describe the pitch vividly," John recalled later. "We were playing the Montreal Expos. I had a 4–0 lead. I threw the pitch and heard this banging sound in my elbow and felt this sharp pain."

John stuck around for two more pitches, walked Bailey, and left the game with a sickening fear that his career might be over. There was a long list of pitchers throughout baseball history to that point whose careers had indeed ended with the kind of elbow injury John had just suffered.

Many years later, Dr. Frank Jobe would joke about the advice given to players with a torn ulnar collateral ligament in their throwing arm.

"We'd tell them to try to get a good job when they got home," Jobe said.

Tendon transfers were not unheard of. But no one had ever tried to do it with a professional athlete, one who made his living flinging baseballs with that arm.

Dr. Jobe was certainly familiar with taking chances. He was drafted at age 18 and joined the 101st Airborne Division of the U.S. Army, where he flew gliders to deliver doctors and medical supplies to the front. When the war ended, he was a decorated soldier with a Bronze Star and a new mission—he went to medical school at Loma Linda University, near Los Angeles, and started a family practice.

After meeting Dr. Robert Kerlan, Jobe did a residency in orthopedics and left family practice to open a clinic with Dr. Kerlan. The two became giants in the emerging field of sports medicine, working with the Dodgers and pitchers like Sandy Koufax, who later teased Jobe that it would be called "Sandy Koufax surgery" if Jobe had thought of trying the procedure a few years sooner.

Jobe said he was first inspired to try the revolutionary elbow surgery by hand surgeons who were transplanting ligaments to restore functionality to the fingers of patients who had suffered severe injuries.

"It wasn't a new idea," Jobe said decades later. "It was just new for the elbow."

After Tommy John left that game against the Montreal Expos, Dr. Jobe examined his elbow and diagnosed a severely sprained UCL. Standard practice at the time was to rest for a month, and hope the pain would subside and the player could go back to playing.

But John wasn't confident a month's rest would heal something that had bothered him for years.

"The arm had always hurt," John said years later. "I was 13, and that's the year you move from the Little League field to the normal baseball field. The pitcher's mound moves back 15 feet [to 60 feet, six inches] and, man, I can remember how much it [his elbow] would swell up."

John had probably spent his entire career with a damaged, possibly torn, UCL in his pitching elbow. He was open to almost anything, and when Jobe proposed a ligament replacement procedure, advising John that there was "probably one in 100" chance that he would return to Major League Baseball, John took the chance.

With a hand surgeon at his side, Dr. Jobe performed the first Tommy John surgery on Tommy John himself. He removed the palmaris tendon—often used in transplant surgeries, because removing it doesn't affect functionality in the hand—from John's right wrist. Jobe drilled holes through the elbow bone and looped the new tendon through it in a figure eight, anchoring it in place.

John returned to the mound in 1976 and pitched until 1989, when he was 46 years old—but his elbow was only 15. He won more games (164) after the surgery than he did before and pitched in three World Series with the Dodgers (1977 and 1978) and Yankees (1981).

In the years since John took the leap with Dr. Jobe, the ligament-replacement procedure became ubiquitous throughout baseball—in the amateur as well as professional ranks.

According to the Kerlan-Jobe Clinic's figures, more than three out of every 10 pitchers on MLB rosters in 2024 had undergone Tommy John surgery at some point. The total number of professional pitchers who returned from the procedure to competitive action had passed 1,200.

"It [has] just prolonged and saved so many careers," said Dr. Tim Kremchek, a long-time member of the Cincinnati Reds' medical staff. "I think it's allowed us to see some of the greatest players in the world continue to play for a long period of time."

For the first 40 years or so, the procedure would be done almost identically. Modifications were made to protect the ulnar nerve and minimize scarring. But the only real decision for the surgeons who followed in Dr. Jobe's footsteps to make was how to loop the new ligament in place.

Recently, there have been significant advances in the surgery. The updated procedure includes the insertion of an internal brace made of bio-compatible material, along with ligament repair rather than a full replacement. Secured to the ulna bone in the forearm and the humerus bone in the upper arm, the brace reinforces the reconstructed ligament.

Dr. Jeffrey R. Dugas has been credited with developing the procedure in 2013, inspired by the use of synthetic supporting tape in ankle ligament repairs. Kansas City Royals pitcher Seth Maness became the first MLB pitcher to undergo the new procedure and return to play. He was back on a mound just under nine months after having the surgery in 2017.

In the baseball world, Texas Rangers team physician Dr. Keith Meister adapted the procedure, adding the internal brace to the traditional UCL replacement surgery. Meister and Dodgers team physician Dr. Neal ElAttrache have been the leading practitioners of the new procedure.

"He and I are both doing the same thing, same philosophy, in adding braided sutures to repair and enhance the existing torn ligament as well as putting in the new graft," ElAttrache said during a 2024 interview with the Associated Press. "So you're getting all the benefits of an augmented, what's called an internal brace, where you're putting sutures in to brace the elbow. I like to put that suture in the native tissue, because then I know it's perfectly anatomic and it'll tighten at exactly the right time."

More and more athletes—including Dodgers right-hander Tyler Glasnow, who had the procedure in 2021 while he was with the Tampa Bay Rays—are getting the internal brace as part of their Tommy John surgery. The modification is supposed to make the ligament more resilient and even allow the athlete to return to competition more quickly.

The pace of Shohei Ohtani's recovery from his second elbow surgery in September 2023 indicates he had the new hybrid procedure this time around. But he has not answered directly when asked if he had the internal brace added this time.

"I'm not, obviously, an expert in the medical field but, I mean, it was a procedure," Ohtani said in December 2023 at his introductory press conference at Dodger Stadium. "I'm not sure what it's called. I know it's completely different from my first time. So I don't know what you want to call it. Probably talk to my doctor about that."

Ohtani's doctor, ElAttrache, did describe the September 2023 surgery on Ohtani as the hybrid procedure involving an internal brace as well as the ligament repair of a traditional Tommy John surgery.

Ohtani's agent, Nez Balelo, said the version of the surgery Ohtani underwent has "no name" but was "completely different than the last time."

Ohtani had his first elbow surgery on October 1, 2018. He returned to action as a designated hitter seven months later but he didn't pitch again until July 2020—a full 20-month recovery, extended by the pandemic delay to MLB's 2020 schedule. He made just two pitching appearances before being shut down with a strained flexor tendon.

At the time, Ohtani expressed frustration, calling his season "pathetic" because of his poor offensive performance and inability to return to the mound.

"[Until then] I could more or less do the things I wanted to do," he told The Ringer in spring 2021. "I'd pretty much never experienced the feeling of wanting to do something but being completely unable to do it."

Ohtani was better prepared for the slow, tedious recovery the second time around.

While he was swinging a bat three months after the surgery and progressing toward a full season as a DH in 2024, he didn't begin a throwing program until late March 2024, six months after the surgery.

The first steps are a light throwing session from a short distance. Throws are limited to 30 or fewer in the early days, gradually increasing.

By May, Ohtani was making 50 throws from 60 feet every other day. By the end of the month, Ohtani reported that he "was able to throw 80 mph" from 60 feet. By the end of June, he was throwing from 90 feet.

"Just continuing to increase the distance and the pitches and just seeing where that goes," Ohtani said.

If Ohtani was showing the necessary patience with the rehab process, he was a long way from taking the mound with the challenge of getting major-league hitters out. Ohtani acknowledged he missed that.

"I think any starting pitcher can tell you that there's a little bit of nervousness going into a game you start," he said in May. "In a sense, I do miss that kind of atmosphere. But right now, I'm really just focusing on progressing every day and really focusing on that."

It was August by the time Ohtani had progressed through the early steps of playing catch, extending out incrementally to throwing from 150 feet and then closing back in to simulate his windup on flat ground and throw with more intensity from the pitching distance of 60 feet.

If rehabbing from Tommy John surgery was Ohtani's day job during those months, he still had a very demanding night job—having an MVP season as the Dodgers' DH. It was a dichotomy that astonished his teammates.

"We can all talk about the stuff on the field and what he does," Freddie Freeman said. "The thing that amazes me is—this man is rehabbing from Tommy John. I don't think people totally understand that. He's out here trying to get his arm and himself ready to throw a baseball. Then he comes in and switches gears and mindsets and goes out and becomes the best hitter in this game. That's what amazes me."

Supervising Ohtani's rehab and getting him ready to pitch in 2025 was the job of a group led by vice president of player performance Brandon McDaniel, head athletic trainer Thomas Albert, strength and conditioning coach Travis Smith, and physical therapist and head of rehabilitation Bernard Li.

McDaniel was part of the Dodgers' pitch to Ohtani during the winter of 2017–18 when Ohtani made the move to MLB. Right away, McDaniel noticed how much more physical the 6-foot-4 Ohtani had become in the years since.

"He's a freight train," McDaniel said after watching Ohtani throw off a mound during his 2024 rehab. "I was fortunate to be in the room in '17 when we did the first round of talking to Shohei. To see that transformation is pretty cool. It's a testament to the work he's put in."

Never having worked with Ohtani before was part of the challenge for the Dodgers' staff guiding him through his recovery in 2024, McDaniel said. Doing no harm to his swing or productivity as a hitter was the biggest challenge.

But what was new for McDaniel, Albert, Smith, and Li was familiar for Ohtani, who had already returned from one elbow surgery.

"He definitely has that vibe," McDaniel said. "He doesn't explicitly say that to us or to me. But you can tell there's a 'I've been here before' kind of mindset. "He's as dialed in with his body as anybody I've ever seen, and knows when anything is off."

That Ohtani could be on a bullpen mound, throwing a 30-pitch bullpen session at nearly full intensity in the afternoon, and then step into the batter's box as the Dodgers' leadoff hitter just an hour or two later was remarkable.

"It's wild to me," McDaniel said, sitting in the visitor's dugout at Chase Field during a September series against the Diamondbacks. "Yesterday, for a 5:00 game, at 3:45 he touched the bump [for a throwing session in the bullpen]. That was some kind of wild to me. And we're not even talking about the game—and then he led off the game with a home run.

"I went to Thomas [Albert] and said, 'Hey we're throwing another bullpen tomorrow.' I'm not superstitious—I'm just a little stitious."

Ohtani's experience made McDaniel wonder if there might be something beneficial about remaining in a competitive environment even as a player rehabs.

"Maybe Shohei playing is also adding to aiding his recovery because he's also put himself in a stressful environment," McDaniel wondered at one point late in the season. "Every other pitcher [recovering from Tommy John surgery] took 12 to 16 months off from ever competing. Shohei has been able to—even though it's not pitching—he has gotten that variable out of the way.

"He's not in a facility by himself. So I think there's a lot of good that has come from this. I'm not going to make any predictions. But I think there's a lot of really cool stuff that we're going to look back and say, 'We need to add components of this to a regular pitcher that isn't a two-way player.'"

Ohtani reached the one-year anniversary of his second elbow surgery on September 19, 2024—the night he went 6-for-6 with three home runs and 10 RBIs to become baseball's first 50-50 player.

"The rehabilitation process isn't entirely fun, and if there are places you advance, there are, of course, places where you also regress," Ohtani said when asked about the coincidence. "I do what I can so that doesn't affect me in the game and I emotionally flip the switch. When I play as a hitter, I am careful to focus fully on that."

From the start of their time with Shohei Ohtani, the Dodgers took the possibility of him pitching in 2024 off the table. But the timing of his surgery in September 2023 and the smoothness of his rehab created a dilemma.

When he started throwing off a mound in August, Ohtani was soon touching 92 mph during his bullpen sessions. The next logical steps would have been for him to face hitters in live batting practice sessions—a staple of the spring training schedule as pitchers prepare for the season.

"Basically, he would be going through his biggest buildups at the beginning or the middle of October," GM Brandon Gomes pointed out.

The Dodgers had other plans for Ohtani at that time of year: leading them through the postseason. Intensifying his rehab as a pitcher at that time would be risky. Ohtani could suffer a minor injury—roll an ankle, strain an oblique muscle—while pitching in rehab that would cost the Dodgers their most dangerous hitter at the most important time of the season.

"It's not good for the now. It's not good for the long term," Gomes said.

It would have been asking a lot, even for an amazing athlete like Ohtani who has multi-tasked at an elite level for years.

"We started throwing when we got back from Korea [in March]," McDaniel said. "Let's just say we took our sweet time and ran [that throwing program] all through the off-season. Then he would go 18 months, 19 months—if you make the playoffs—without a break. On the mound, it would put him in a really difficult situation.

"Stress is stress. I personally don't believe your brain recognizes you're throwing a baseball. Your brain recognizes stress.... We've had a chance to ramp this thing up and we're going to get to a point where we say, 'Okay, this is where we maintain,' because we don't want to stop. But at the same time, we can't put stress on top of playoff games.

"'Hey, I need you to lead off tonight. We're playing in the NLCS and at 2:00 I need you to throw a live BP.'... What if he takes a comebacker? Or he slips on the mound? Everything has to be balanced with any progression we look at with a player. This adds a pretty unique component to it. Hey, we can't risk something incidental happening. We can't risk the comebacker. We can't risk a slip. We can't risk a shoe blowing out. Whatever it might be. That happens. That's part of doing business."

McDaniel acknowledged that Ohtani's rehab went "as seamless and as easy as possible for how hard the actual rehab is." Observers couldn't help but fantasize about a dream scenario— Shohei Ohtani coming in from the bullpen to close out a World Series championship for the Dodgers, just as he had for Team Japan in the 2023 World Baseball Classic.

"He's not pitching for us this year. He's not," Gomes said in August. "There's no world where he's pitching for us this postseason."

Dr. Neal ElAttrache—the man who performed both of Ohtani's elbow surgeries—was certainly not in favor of it.

"It's not really a good idea for anyone coming back from elbow or shoulder surgery to make their return to competition in the postseason," ElAttrache said. "There are no minor-league games to get rehab starts for a return to competition at this time of year, so their first competition would be in postseason, high-stress conditions. Not a good idea for the player or the team."

But the idea persisted in the media, even as Dodgers president of baseball operations Andrew Friedman tried to dismiss the speculation.

"We aren't even thinking about that right now," Friedman said in late September. "Again, this is, like, January for him [as a pitcher]. He's just barely a year out from Tommy John. To me, he's not really an option."

It was only a topic because of how seamlessly Ohtani and the Dodgers' staff had handled his rehab, even while he was playing every day at DH. There was never any indication of a bad day or missed marker along the way.

"Clearly, it's seamless for him," Dodgers pitching coach Mark Prior said. "I think we've all said it—it's definitely a unique challenge. I think everybody at this point has said any adjective to describe the way he goes about his business. But it's pretty impressive."

Prior echoed McDaniel in wondering how much benefit Ohtani's rehab might be getting from his ability to still compete in games as a hitter.

"Maybe it's a good thing that he has the ability to disconnect, compartmentalize, and go hit and do all the things he's doing on the offensive side," Prior said. "Where normally as pitchers, you're kind of ingrained with the same monotony. You can kind of get bogged down in every ache, soreness, the good, bad, [or] indifferent throw. Maybe it gives him a chance to actually be free and relaxed.

"He can do something that's pretty remarkable. But he takes everything in stride and he's very meticulous in what he wants to do, and makes sure he puts himself in a position to accomplish that."

But Shohei Ohtani was not ready to reject the idea of pitching before the end of 2024. Instead, he said there had been "no conversation" about him pitching in 2024 but a meeting was planned for the end of the regular season "to discuss the overall rehab progression."

Asked if he thought he could be physically ready to pitch at some time during a playoff run, Ohtani replied with a sly smile as he said in Japanese, "I am not sure."

The meeting eventually took place as the season wound down and the Dodgers prepared for the postseason. It was not about getting Ohtani ready to pitch in the postseason, Friedman insisted. It was about settling on an optimal schedule that would get Ohtani ready to pitch in 2025.

"The meeting is about his rehab progression and timing for how to get him ready for next year—which has always been planned to get into," Friedman said. "If you strip away what's going on with the Dodgers, right now [in late September] he's thrown about five bullpens, which is the equivalent of January, late January in his progression [if he was going through a normal preseason buildup], and October lines up at some point middle to late for live BPs like pitchers do when they come to spring training.

"The question is whether to do those then [in October] or do them in November, but make sure he has enough shutdown time before the start of the following year. This has been on our radar as something to talk about since spring training.

"The whole meeting is about how we handle his rehab to have him in the best position to be ready to go in '25 while also taking the least amount of toll on him in '24, because he will have an important job in October as it is.... Okay, if you suspend [his rehab] then and do it in November, is that enough time, or do you ramp him up and have him a little bit later [at the start of the 2025 season]? That's the stuff we have to get into."

The outcome of that meeting between team officials, medical staff (including Dr. Neal ElAttrache), Ohtani, and his representatives was that Ohtani scaled back his throwing program during the Dodgers' postseason run. He continued to play catch and throw before games on an intermittent basis. But facing hitters was postponed until after the season.

"I plan to continue with the rehab process, to the extent that it wouldn't affect the performance on the field, because the games that we're going to play [in October] will be more important," Ohtani said after the meeting. "I think it's important to keep myself fresh and be game ready."

Like so much with Ohtani, it was unknown territory with no precedents to follow.

"It's something that's there's not a clear answer to," Friedman said. "So the question is, what is the prudent route, and how does his body feel as we continue through his progression?"

The Dodgers got one clear answer when Ohtani suffered a left shoulder injury during the World Series—he will not be ready to start the 2025 season on time as a pitcher.

Ohtani suffered a partial dislocation of his non-throwing shoulder while sliding in Game 2 against the Yankees. He played through the injury for the remainder of the Series but underwent arthroscopic surgery days later to repair a torn labrum in the shoulder.

While the surgery is not expected to have any significant impact on Ohtani's pitching in 2025, his rehab will probably last long enough to push back Ohtani's return to pitching.

A late return to pitching in 2025 would disappoint an entire country. The Dodgers will open the 2025 season with two regular-season games against the Chicago Cubs at the Tokyo Dome on March 18 and 19—raising the tantalizing possibility of Ohtani and Yoshinobu Yamamoto starting those games for the Dodgers.

"We're just going to make sure we're checking every box to make sure he's in the best possible position health-wise," Dodgers GM Brandon Gomes said. "And then whatever falls out of that smart, methodical process will be what it is."

There are other issues that come with Ohtani's return to two-way status in 2025 that will require careful handling by the Dodgers. For one, how will the Dodgers integrate Ohtani into a starting rotation that dissolved due to injuries each of the past two seasons?

Both Ohtani and Yoshinobu Yamamoto will be given a minimum of five days' rest between starts (four days is considered "normal" rest), making a six-man rotation a necessity. (The Angels did the same when Ohtani was in their rotation.) That will require inventory. As the 2024 season ended, the Dodgers had a long list of pitchers who will be coming off injuries and/ or surgeries in 2025—Tyler Glasnow, Tony Gonsolin, Clayton Kershaw, and Dustin May, as well as young prospects Emmet Sheehan, River Ryan, and Kyle Hurt. After a strong rookie season, Gavin Stone underwent shoulder surgery in October and will be unavailable until 2026. Walker Buehler and Jack Flaherty would become free agents after the 2024 season.

"I don't know," Friedman said honestly when asked what a Dodgers' rotation with Ohtani in it would look like. "We'll have a rough plan with outs [ways to pivot], be around it, assess it, see how he's bouncing back [after starts]. There's a lot we cannot know sitting here today, so we're not going to pretend to. Just have as much flexibility as we can, and as we're learning more and more actionable information, then we'll figure out what that looks like."

The Dodgers expect to have "the benefit of pitching depth" around Ohtani in 2025, Gomes said.

"He won't ever have to go on regular [rest]," Gomes said. "There are compounding effects from that. Going into the season, we'll sit down and have a conversation about what it's going to look like. We're obviously not going to throw him 220 innings next year. [Ohtani topped out at 166 innings with the Angels in 2022]. It's just trying to figure out how to thoughtfully lay these things out to the best of our ability."

There are "a lot of benefits" to being able to carry Ohtani as a two-way player in 2025, Friedman added.

"You can have a 13-man pitching staff—and then Shohei," he said. "And the rule change from a couple years ago, where if he starts the game as a pitcher and gets taken out, he remains as the DH. I view all those roster rules as just beneficial."

Looming over Ohtani's return to pitching in 2025 will be the question of how it will impact his performance at the plate. As his historic season progressed in 2024, it became obvious that being able to focus on just being a DH freed up the best version of Ohtani as a hitter—and as a baserunner.

"I don't know," Friedman said when asked if Ohtani's offense will drop off in 2025 if he is a two-way player. "It's hard for me to fathom. This is all unprecedented stuff."

Dodgers hitting coach Robert Van Scoyoc starts his answer with the same three words—"I don't know"—when asked how a return to two-player status in 2025 might affect Ohtani's offensive production.

"Obviously, I haven't seen it. I haven't seen him pitch and all that, and how that affects everything," Van Scoyoc said.

"He's pretty good at compartmentalizing everything. It's hard to say. Hitting goes in waves. Who's to say if he ends up having a better year it wouldn't have happened. It's impossible to scale."

Like Brandon McDaniel, Dodgers assistant hitting coach Aaron Bates also thinks Ohtani's work as a pitcher benefits him as a hitter.

"I have this theory. I don't know. We'll see next year if it's proven or not," Bates said. "If he were to stop pitching next year, for example, I think it [his production as a hitter] would slowly taper off, because I think those workouts and pitching actually help him a lot. Even mentally it helps him, so I think you're getting this elite version this year with just hitting. I think the pitching side of things—one, it's a mental break from hitting, just in general. And two, you look at all these major-league pitchers and how strong their legs are, the force they generate. That relates to Shohei's swing.

"So if he were to stop pitching all of a sudden, it would be interesting to see if maintaining the workouts as if he was a pitcher—because that leg strength he has is so phenomenal. I think he has a lot of it because he has to pitch or he has to build himself up to pitch.… You have good seasons and bad seasons, numbers-wise. But I think he's just going to continue to get better as a hitter as he learns himself more. But I don't anticipate the physical toll on his body, taking away from his hitting."

Surprisingly, Bates said Ohtani told him he did not change his routine as a hitter in 2024. There was no added work despite the extra time afforded him without bullpen sessions and pitching maintenance.

"He's maintained the same routine, is what he's said, as when he's pitching in hitting right now," Bates said. "So it's not like he's done something more in hitting now that he's been able to spend more time on it. So I think next year it will be a smooth transition. If anything, he might be physically a little more tired. But at the same time, he's working out more as a pitcher. So I'm not expecting a big dropoff. Maybe in basestealing."

That is a consensus among Dodgers staff. Ohtani is not likely to run as often or as aggressively in 2025 as he did while stealing a shocking 59 bases during his 50-50 season in 2024.

"I'm just never going to put anything past this guy," Freddie Freeman said. "Maybe that won't be the same.

"I don't know what the dropoff is [when he returns to being a two-way player] because a dropoff from those [2024] numbers are still probably going to be the best player in the league. It's not really a dropoff because every year is going to be different. As much as we all want to hit .320, .315, .330 every year, there are ebbs and flows. Things go on in your career. You just try to do the best with what you've got. Is he going to do 50-50 again? I don't know. I'm not going to put it past him."

Dodgers veteran Clayton Kershaw said he is "excited" to see Ohtani pitch in 2025.

"I always thought he was good at pitching," Kershaw said. "I think we all feel like, gosh, I hope it doesn't take away from what he does offensively. But it probably has to a little bit."

Dodgers manager Dave Roberts said he believes there are things Ohtani has been able to do with "a heightened focus on just hitting" in 2024 that can persist when he returns to being a two-way player.

"There's a commitment to being a better hitter, to controlling the strike zone," Roberts said. "And then we will see next year, with that same mindset, layering on the pitching part. To add the pitching part—what a unique, generational player."

Ohtani seemed to have that same expectation—that a return to pitching won't wash away the improvements he made as a hitter through 2024.

"I think it's unquestionable that I'm able to recover properly because there's less of a workload," Ohtani said. "Plus, as I pile up experience year after year, I'm growing as a hitter."

Dodgers hitting coach Robert Van Scoyoc takes his own pragmatic view of what impact Ohtani's returning to two-way play might have.

"Like everyone here, I just want to win, and when he's pitching he's one of the best pitchers in the game," Van Scoyoc said. "So helping us win is only a good thing. Whatever unintended consequences that has on his hitting, we'll deal with that at that time. But it's only positive if he's pitching for us."

Ohtani's career has already been so unique, trying to predict how his two-way talents play out in the future is kind of pointless, GM Brandon Gomes said.

"Is he going to go 50-50 for 10 years? I would never bet against Kersh and I would never bet against Shohei," Gomes said. "What he is capable of doing just from an offensive standpoint, I think, is incredibly valuable. Then layer on the pitching.… Our full expectation is that he is going to pitch and be very good."

Dodgers president of baseball operations Andrew Friedman rejected the idea that Ohtani has to return to being a two-way player—or has to continue pitching for a significant part of the next 10 years—in order to justify the largest contract ever given to a professional athlete. The prospect of being "stuck" with a $700 million DH if Ohtani has to stop pitching for some reason is not one Friedman considers.

"I don't look at it that way," he said. "I have a lot of confidence that he is going to pitch and be really good at it while maintaining a really high level in the [batter's] box. I don't think it's as simple as X number of innings [as a pitcher] therefore makes it good. I think it's taking it year by year and doing everything we can do to be as good as we can be that year. In my mind, sitting here right now, that's going to be with him doing both as far as we can see out. If we ever need to adjust, we will together. And if that happens, I'm very confident that I won't then regret the deal.

"I don't know [how long Ohtani can be a two-way player]. But the thing that I've learned from watching from afar and now being way more up close and personal is that I wouldn't bet against him. I know that he is determined to do it for a long time and I certainly would not take the other side of that bet."

For his part, Mookie Betts just wants to see what it looks like to have a two-way teammate.

"I'm genuinely excited," he said on his podcast. "It's going to be a national holiday the first day he pitches [for the Dodgers]."

Chapter 8

50-50 Club of One

From the moment it became obvious that Shohei Ohtani would spend the 2024 season as a one-way player—rehabbing to pitch in 2025 but focusing his time, skills, and physical resources on offensive production as he never had before—it was apparent his unique combination of power and speed could result in some unique numbers.

Ohtani hit a career-high 46 home runs during his first MVP season with the Angels, in 2021. He also struck out 189 times that year and batted just .257. Undoubtedly, he had become a better hitter in the years since.

During his second MVP season, in 2023, Ohtani hit 44 home runs while batting .304 and lowering his strikeout rate from 29.6 to 23.6. In both cases, he was still operating with the Angels' support system, one not nearly as sophisticated as the hitting group the Dodgers put together.

"Sho is a self-starter, so I don't think it matters what is available to him," Dodgers hitting coach Robert Van Scoyoc said carefully of the difference in resources between the Angels and Dodgers coaching staffs. "I think he's going to be good either way. Obviously with the long-term relationship that we're going to have with him, I don't think we've shied away from coaching him. 'Hey, this is what we've got. This is how you get better.' Just having those conversations and knowing that we're going to work together for the foreseeable future makes it easier to coach him."

In 2024, Ohtani had hit seven home runs by the end of April and added seven more in May. He surged in June after moving into the leadoff spot and reached the All-Star break with 29 home runs. The Dodgers' franchise record of 49 home runs (Shawn Green, in 2001) was clearly within reach for a healthy Ohtani.

If Ohtani's power was obvious, another attribute was the one his teammates would often point to as most surprising during his first season with the Dodgers.

"His speed around the bases," Dodgers assistant hitting coach Aaron Bates said. "I didn't know how fast he was. You knew he was fleet of foot. But watching him run was like a deer."

Dodgers first-base coach Clayton McCullough knew Ohtani was "fast" and "long," with strides that chewed up ground as he ran the bases. What he didn't know before 2024 was how eager Ohtani was to improve that aspect of his game.

"It started in spring training," McCullough said. "He spent a lot of time in the off-season and this spring with [strength and conditioning coach] Travis Smith on running mechanics, his acceleration. That was a real point of emphasis. It was, 'Yeah, I'm fast. Can we get faster in those first 10 feet?' That usually makes a big difference. Can we accelerate quicker? Because he's big, there's a lot of parts to get moving."

Among McCullough's duties is film study with Ohtani, looking for pitchers' "tells."

"The difference between a pickoff and a delivery can be this subtle little move," McCullough said. "That's kind of what we do a lot going into a series. We'll have some things we go over. We'll watch some things. It'll be, 'Hey, this is what I see. Do you see it?' Sometimes things stand out and it's 'If you see this during the game, it's going to be really good.' Other times, the times are going to be this. Are you going to be able to outrun the combination of this pitcher and this catcher?"

Not having worked with Ohtani during his years with the Angels, McCullough couldn't say if any of this was unique to the circumstances in 2024. But a couple things were.

Rules changes in 2023 boosted stolen bases, making it easier for runners by increasing the size of the bases themselves and limiting pitchers to two disengagements (pickoff attempts) per batter. There were more stolen bases in 2023 than any season since 1987.

And then there was Ohtani's expectation of spending the 2024 season as a one-way player, able to contribute only offensively.

"It seemed like it was a conscious effort on his part coming into this year, knowing that 'I'm only going to be an offensive player this year. This is going to be a chance to push that a little bit more without having to worry about recovery or days when I'm pitching,'" McCullough said. "I think that's probably a big part in his mind. I don't know if he has a number or set a goal. That I don't know.

"People have asked me during the season—how many [bases can he steal]? You know what—I would never set a limit on this guy.... However many it ends up being, I'm just proud of how diligent he has been in his preparation. Like everything else he does, he puts time into studying information beforehand."

Ohtani ran often enough to steal 15 bases in his first 70 games. But that was while batting second in the Dodgers' lineup behind Mookie Betts, which somewhat limited his opportunities.

"I don't know if he set out this year to steal that many bases. That's just how it came about," Dodgers assistant hitting coach Aaron Bates speculated. "He got to 30 and it was, 'Oh, hey—I can do this,' because he stole a lot late [in the season]. It wasn't like he came out of the gate and he was running. Then it became a thing and they knew he was going and he was still going. I think he just saw it [stealing 50 bases] was within reach."

The starter's pistol went off in July.

He nearly matched his total from the first three months (16) with 12 successful steals in 14 attempts. He matched his previous career-high with his 26th steal against the Houston Astros on July 27, just 106 games into the Dodgers' season. In the same game, he hit a 443-foot home run that left his bat at 118.7 mph—a power-and-speed combo rarely seen.

With a three-steal game against the Oakland A's on August 3, he reached 31 steals in just 111 games.

Of the 70 30-30 seasons in baseball history, Ohtani was the fourth-fastest player to reach the milestone, matching José Canseco, who also did it in 111 games, for the Oakland A's in 1988.

"He was really focusing on keeping his body in a good spot and using his legs, which he was really excited to be able to run free [as a one-way player]," Dodgers manager Dave Roberts said. "You obviously knew he was going to hit homers. I do think 40-40 was something that was on his radar from spring training."

Roberts said he spoke with Ohtani about stealing bases during spring training and made it clear he was "all in for him being aggressive and picking the right spots," even though he would be batting in front of Freddie Freeman.

"I think that was kind of something that allowed him the freedom to then work on his jumps and his speed," Roberts said. "Obviously [he's] not worrying about pitching, so now he can sort of just let it go and empty the tank offensively. I think that's a part of it as well."

There was another added element fueling Ohtani in 2024, Roberts said.

"He's in a pennant race now, and I don't think he's been in a pennant race in his big-league career," Roberts said, aware the Angels had been nowhere near a playoff spot, let alone a pennant race, during Ohtani's six years there. "So his enhanced focus is not a surprise to me. And he's trying to dominate on every margin."

Ohtani wouldn't acknowledge a 40-40 season as a goal, saying only that he focuses on "having a good process" and if that results in more home runs and more stolen bases "and other aspects of the at-bats, like moving guys over or being selective and choosing the walks—those are things that I value a lot."

"No goals, per se," he said.

In his 118th game of the season, Ohtani drew a walk in the second inning, then stole second and third. It gave him 35 stolen bases along with 37 home runs for the season. Only one player in history had reached the 35-35 marks in fewer games played. (Eric Davis did it in 115 games for the Cincinnati Reds during the 1987 season.)

As he was clicking past the historic markers, though, Ohtani was going through one of his worst slumps of the season. Despite having Mookie Betts back in the lineup and hitting behind him, Ohtani started August just 10 for his first 61 (.164), dropping his average for the season under .300 on August 11.

"I think the plate discipline is just not what it is when he's right," Dave Roberts said. "His walk percentage, I'm sure, in the last three weeks is considerably down. I think the swing decisions aren't as good as they have been."

Roberts dismissed the idea of Ohtani being fatigued from playing every day.

"I wouldn't think when you're taking four at-bats a night as a DH, fatigue should be factor. I don't think so," he said.

Roberts was more open to the suggestion that Ohtani might be trying to do too much with each at-bat—either because of the pressure to chase history or because of his inexperience with pursuing a playoff spot.

As his slump persisted with a 5-for-30 road trip to Milwaukee and St. Louis, Ohtani said his issues were mechanical.

"I think having the right posture when I'm looking at the pitcher is something that's really important," he said. "I feel like it's a little off. But in the meantime, when things are off, there's also something I can make up for by having a better approach at the plate."

Ohtani said it was all about the simplest thing a hitter has to do—"swinging at strikes."

Ohtani was making progress when the Dodgers opened a nine-game homestand against the Seattle Mariners on August 19. He had four hits in the three games against the Mariners, including a triple, and he stole two bases.

That put him at 39 home runs and 39 stolen bases for the season. He got one half of the milestone combo in the fourth inning against the Tampa Bay Rays on August 23, stealing second base after reaching on an infield single.

Ohtani grounded out in his next two at-bats but the game went into the ninth inning tied.

Rays right-hander Manuel Rodriguez hit Will Smith with a pitch to start the inning, then gave up a single to Tommy Edman. Miguel Rojas bunted both runners into scoring position. Gavin Lux couldn't get the winning run across, but Rays manager Kevin Cash had seen enough of Rodriguez and brought in left-hander Colin Poche to face pinch-hitter Max Muncy.

Poche struggled with his control and walked Muncy on five pitches to load the bases and bring up Ohtani. The confrontation didn't last long. Poche left a first-pitch slider over the plate and Ohtani drove it high into the night. It came down just beyond the reach of center fielder Jose Siri. The ball landed in the hands of a fan who had enough forethought to bring a glove to the game—but he fumbled the big opportunity, letting the ball bounce back onto the field.

With that, Ohtani became the sixth player in baseball history to hit 40 home runs and steal 40 bases in the same season. The dramatic, history-making home run came in his 126th game of the season, the fastest 40-40 season in history, 21 games faster than Washington's Alfonso Soriano, in 2006.

"One of my top memorable moments," Ohtani said. "I hope that I can do more and make more memorable moments."

A walkoff grand slam to reach 40-40 is a pretty high bar. But Ohtani surpassed it when that milestone got close.

"I mean, 40-40, same game, walkoff grand slam," Dave Roberts gushed afterward. "Man, if there was a script, that couldn't have been written any better. Shohei just never ceases to amaze."

The "M-V-P! M-V-P!" chants had barely died down when Ohtani was being asked about the next potential target—an unprecedented 50-50 season. The Dodgers' season had 33 games left for Ohtani to get there. Roberts declared it a possibility.

"It is," he said. "With this guy and over a month of baseball left, I think anything's possible."

With their lead in the division over the hard-charging Diamondbacks and Padres fluctuating between three and four games, Ohtani professed to be more focused on securing the NL West.

"I think the most important thing is to be able to contribute to winning the game," Ohtani said of pursuing the next personal milestone. "And obviously, the closer I get to 50-50, the more I'm contributing to the team winning. So if that's how it is, then I'm happy with that."

Just five days later, Ohtani had to be happy with playing second fiddle perhaps for the only time all season.

He was upstaged by his dog, Decoy.

Though his name was kept a mystery for some time, the young pup, a Dutch Kooikerhondje by breed, walked the red carpet in spirit at the All-Star Game when Ohtani wore a brown suit featuring Decoy's face on the suit jacket lining. Later in the year, Ohtani occasionally wore cleats with Decoy's image on them.

On August 28, Decoy had his biggest moment. He joined Ohtani on the field for pregame festivities tied to Ohtani's second bobblehead day of the season. Like the first, it drew throngs of fans who lined up hours before game time in order to make sure they got their promotional bobblehead, this time featuring both Ohtani and Decoy.

"I was surprised as well when I came to the park with my family," Ohtani said of the pregame excitement. "I wasn't really aware of the situation. I thought it was some other special event going on."

When the big moment arrived, Ohtani carried Decoy (wearing his own customized No. 17 Dodgers jersey) out to the pitcher's mound. Setting the ball down on the rubber, Ohtani told Decoy to stay, then trotted behind home plate. In a crouch, Ohtani signaled for Decoy to deliver the first pitch. He scooped the ball in his mouth and trotted straight to his owner, delivering a strike...and a high-five.

A few minutes later, Ohtani hit the fifth pitch he saw in his first at-bat over the wall in right field for a home run.

Still, it was the first-pitch video that went viral, making Decoy an even bigger star as the deliverer of possibly the cutest first pitch in baseball history.

Ohtani said he had practiced for three weeks with Decoy—"We even did a dry run here at the stadium," he said.

"We just kind of had a fun exercise," he said, promising Decoy a "special snack" for pulling off a perfect first pitch.

Ohtani said the most nervous he was during his debut season with the Dodgers was during Decoy's big moment.

Ohtani ended August with a .235 average, by far his lowest for any calendar month in 2024. He still managed to hit 12 home runs, tied with June for his best month, and steal 15 bases, good enough to keep a 50-50 season in play.

Ohtani hadn't been caught on a steal attempt since July 22. According to statistician Sarah Langs, no player in baseball history had hit 12 or more home runs in a month and gone 15-for-15 (or better) in steal attempts in a month—any month—over the course of an entire career. Ohtani did it in the *same* month.

As August ended and the season rolled into September, the Dodgers took three out of four games from Arizona at Chase Field, reducing the Diamondbacks as a threat in the division.

In the second game of the series, Ohtani, Mookie Betts, and Freddie Freeman led off the game with consecutive home runs. It was the 16th time in franchise history the Dodgers had hit three consecutive home runs—but the first time it happened to start a game.

With even more history still in front of him, Ohtani revisited his past.

The Dodgers went to Anaheim for a two-game series against the Angels on September 3 and 4. Ohtani reflected on his six years with the Angels that were filled with personal achievements but almost no team success.

"Me personally, I had seasons that were good but also seasons in which I was injured and couldn't play or couldn't pitch," he said. "If I had been able to contribute to the maximum, I think there are parts that would have been different."

When asked if things might have been different had the Angels matched the offer on the table during his free agency in December 2023, Ohtani shrugged.

"I'm just thankful and grateful for the teams that ended up offering a contract. That's the reflection of what they think about me," Ohtani said. "In reality, I wasn't made an offer [by the Angels] so I can't say [if he would have accepted]. In reality, I'm doing my best with this team and I'm doing my best with the goal of winning the World Series. I think I'm fine with that."

More than fine with it, Ohtani was enjoying his first chance to play meaningful games in September.

"Personally, it's my first time being able to experience being at this spot in the standings and being able to play against other division rivals who are trying to take the spot as well," Ohtani said. "So personally, it's very exciting."

Dodgers manager Dave Roberts said he suspected the series in Anaheim would provide "closure" for that part of Ohtani's career—and validation of his decision to leave for a championship contender like the Dodgers.

"I think it's going to be special for everyone," Roberts said. "Just speaking for Shohei, it might be a little bit of closure in the sense of he had such a great time here in Anaheim. So the fans will get a chance to show their appreciation, gratitude. I think for him it'll be a nice moment. But I know he's excited to be a Dodger and competing for a championship."

On their way to the worst record in franchise history (63–99), the Angels still sold out both games against the Dodgers (with the help of a healthy number of Dodgers fans).

The team honored Ohtani with a tribute video on the scoreboard when Ohtani visited during the preseason Freeway Series. Now playing games that counted, there was no tribute video, just a simple graphic on the scoreboard listing his achievements with the Angels as he stepped in for his first official at-bat as a visitor at Angel Stadium.

On a different part of the scoreboard, "Fun Facts" are listed under the batter's name. For Ohtani, it read, "Used to work here"—slyly funny but probably not fun for his former team's fans.

After the game, Ohtani called the return to Anaheim "special for me" but remained focused on winning. He contributed to that the first night with an RBI triple in the third inning, then was intentionally walked in the 10th inning. Mookie Betts responded with a three-run home run.

"You know, they walked Sho to get to me and I was just like, 'Alright,'" Betts said.

The Angels got their revenge with a lopsided win on the second night, starting a slump that saw the Dodgers lose six of their next nine games, including the first two of a four-game series in Atlanta that had the potential to tighten the NL West race again.

On the first day in Atlanta, right-hander Tyler Glasnow was expected to throw a simulated game, giving the Dodgers hope that he would be able to return to their rotation in time for the postseason.

But he never even made it to the mound at Truist Park. While he was warming up in the bullpen, Glasnow felt renewed pain in his elbow and shut it down. An MRI revealed a sprained elbow and Glasnow did not pitch again in 2024. The next day, his locker was cleared out, and he was gone.

To many of the Dodgers, it felt like the final straw in a season-long avalanche of injuries and setbacks. Before the third game of the four-game series, Roberts gathered the team to discuss the "woe is us" attitude he felt in the air.

"And that's just not who we are," Roberts said.

He reminded the team that they still had the best record in the National League, still controlled their playoff destiny, and still had enough talent to win a championship.

"That was basically Doc's message," Andrew Friedman said later. "'Hey, look—we can focus on who's gotten hurt. But take a moment and look around at the talent in this room. Let's focus on that.'"

It was a moment that "turned our season around," Max Muncy would say later.

"Not from the team but from the outside—everybody was panicking because we had a lot of injuries. We lost a lot of pitchers," Teoscar Hernández said. "And it was one time that we felt like we were down as a team. And one meeting changed everything.

"We realized that we have the potential, that we have the players, that we're still the Dodgers, and we can do special things with the people we have.... It was just a meeting to put everybody's head up again and just keep pushing until we win everything."

The Dodgers won that night and won 11 of their final 14 games, including taking two out of three from the Padres to put them away in the division. They would finish with the best record in baseball.

There was still history to be made, however.

"I think that he wants to be the greatest player to ever play this game," Roberts said of Ohtani pursuing the first 50-50 season. "And when you start doing things like that, then you're certainly staking your claim."

From Atlanta, the Dodgers traveled to Miami for a three-game series against the lowly Marlins. In the opener, Ohtani hit his 48th home run of the season—but also struck out three times, an indication that he might be pressing to reach the historic mark.

In the Atlanta series, he went without a home run or stolen base for four consecutive games for the first time since early June.

"No pressure," Ohtani said. "Just trying to maintain quality at-bats no matter the situation—something I've been trying to do over the course of the season."

The 48th home run pulled him within one of matching Shawn Green's single-season franchise record. Coupled with his 48 stolen bases, Ohtani had already reached a double no other player had before.

"I don't think he's feeling pressure. I do think that it's front of mind," Dave Roberts said. "And I do feel that's somewhat natural. I think he just wants to get it over with. But with the fact that he's still trying to compete and help us win baseball games."

Ohtani didn't contribute much in a win over the Marlins in the second game of the series. He was 1-for-5 with a single and did steal a base, his 49th of the season.

History was finally within reach and Shohei Ohtani was ready to grab it.

Ohtani led off the final game of the series by ripping a 2-and-2 changeup from Marlins starter Edward Cabrera 114.6 mph into right-center field for a double. It was the hardest-hit ball of the game, the first of five Ohtani would hit at least 105 mph off the bat.

After Mookie Betts popped out, Freddie Freeman drew a walk. With Will Smith at the plate, Ohtani and Freeman took off on a double steal, Ohtani just beating the throw to third base from catcher Nick Fortes with a slide to the outfield side of the base.

It was his 50th steal of the season.

An inning later, Ohtani came up with two on and two out and got another changeup from Cabrera. He ripped this one into right field for an RBI single. With an exit velocity of 97.1 mph, it was Ohtani's softest contact of the night. With Betts at the plate, Ohtani took off for second and stole his 51st base of the season.

Cabrera wasn't around when Ohtani came up yet again in the third inning. Chris Taylor had just driven in the Dodgers' third run of the inning and fifth of the game, bringing up Ohtani with runners at the corners and two outs.

Marlins reliever Anthony Veneziano went to a full count on Ohtani, then left a fastball up over the plate. Ohtani ripped it (105.1 mph) into the left-center gap this time. It one-hopped the wall for a two-run double but Ohtani kept going, trying for a triple. He was out on a relay throw from center fielder Kyle Stowers to shortstop Xavier Edwards to third baseman Connor Norby.

"He almost got a cycle in four at-bats," Dodgers shortstop Miguel Rojas marveled after the game. "If the cutoff man throws the ball away a little bit, he's got a cycle in four at-bats."

Ohtani never did get his second cycle (he did it in 2019)—because all he did the rest of the night was hit home runs.

Three at-bats, three different pitchers, three home runs.

In the sixth inning, Marlins reliever George Soriano was the victim. He left an 0-and-1 slider over the plate and Ohtani sent it on a 111.2-mph journey 438 feet over the wall in right-center field for a two-run home run, Ohtani's 49th of the season.

The game was on its way to laugher status an inning later when Ohtani came up to face reliever Mike Baumann with a chance to make history. For the first time, officials signaled to home-plate umpire Dan Iassogna to put specially marked baseballs into play. If Ohtani homered, Major League Baseball wanted to be able to verify and authenticate the lucky fan who collected the baseball.

Mookie Betts was asked later if his teammates were afraid to say anything to Ohtani about hitting his 50th home run of the season. Baseball has always had room for superstition. Pitchers in the midst of a no-hitter, for example, are left alone in the dugout by tradition, out of fear a teammate could somehow jinx the endeavor.

"No," Betts said. "I don't think you can jinx greatness like that."

No—but you can intentionally walk it.

With runners on second and third and the Marlins already trailing 11–3, Marlins manager Skip Schumaker could have waved Ohtani on to first base and avoided the historic confrontation.

On the broadcast, cameras captured Schumaker responding to members of his coaching staff who appeared to be advising just that.

"Fuck that," even an amateur lip-reader could see Schumaker saying. "I've got too much respect for this guy for that to happen."

This exchange was noted across the field in the Dodgers' dugout.

"A lot of us actually looked into the opposing dugout, and I think a lot of the coaches were telling Skip, 'Hey, we should walk him here,'" Dodgers third baseman Max Muncy said. "I have no idea what was actually said over there but that's how it looked. You could kind of tell Skip was, 'I can't do that.'

"So, tip of the cap to Skip right there for letting him hit."

After the game, Schumaker was asked about his decision to pitch to Ohtani in that moment and earned even more respect for his answer.

"I think that's a bad move—baseball-wise, karma-wise, baseball gods–wise. You go after him and see if you can get him out," Schumaker said. "I think out of respect for the game we were going to go after him. He hit the home run. That's just part of the deal. He's hit 50 of them.

"It was a good day for baseball. But a bad day for the Marlins."

Ohtani fouled off the first two pitches from Baumann to fall behind in the count, then took a curveball in the dirt that allowed the Dodgers' 12th run to score. Baumann's next pitch was another curveball. Not a good one.

Ohtani reached out and drove it into the seats in right-center field for his 50th home run of the season, erupting with emotion and looking toward his teammates in the Dodgers' dugout before starting his trot around the bases.

"Just happy, relieved, and very respectful to the peers and everybody that came before that played this sport of baseball," Ohtani said through his interpreter after the game.

"If I'm being honest, it was something that I wanted to get over as soon as possible, because the balls were being exchanged every time I was up to bat. So it was something that I wanted to get over with."

But it wasn't over with.

On their way to a season-high 20 runs, the Dodgers scored six more in the ninth inning. The Marlins resorted to sending two different position players to the mound to pitch. Ohtani hit a three-run home run off the first, Vidal Bruján, a utilityman by trade making his second pitching appearance of the season.

The exclamation mark on Ohtani's historic night came in at 68.3 mph out of Bruján's hand and left Ohtani's bat at 113.6 mph, traveling 440 feet into the stands.

"I think he was just feeling good, feeling sexy, and just knew, like, 'I'm about to do this today,'" Betts said of Ohtani inaugurating the 50-50 club. "I mean, he could have had four homers today. I'm at a loss for words."

The rest of Ohtani's teammates were not. The words gushed forth in the postgame locker room, the Dodgers celebrating both Ohtani's accomplishment and the team having clinched a postseason berth.

Dodgers manager Dave Roberts offered a champagne toast after the game, recognizing both achievements.

"This is a game that has been played for over 200 years, and he [Ohtani] has done something that's never been done in this game," Roberts said.

Ohtani was also about to do something else he had never done before. Coming into the game, he had played 850 MLB games without making a postseason appearance, more than any other active player. That drought was going to end.

With a career-high six hits (a single, two doubles, and three home runs), a franchise-record 10 RBIs, and two stolen bases, he became the first player in MLB history to combine six hits, three homers, 10 RBIs, and two steals in a single game.

"Take the season out of it—today was probably the single best offensive game I've ever seen," Muncy said. "What did he have—six hits, 10 RBIs, three home runs? And don't forget he had two or three stolen bases today also—yeah, why not? That's insane."

Gavin Lux picked up the "greatest baseball game of all time" line.

"It has to be," Lux said. "There's no way. It's ridiculous. I've never seen anybody do that, even in Little League."

That his 50-50 game came at Miami's loanDepot Park, site of the 2023 World Baseball Classic championship game where Ohtani clinched Team Japan's victory, was not lost on him.

"I've had perhaps the most memorable moments here in my career," Ohtani said. "And this stadium has become one of my favorite stadiums."

"It was remarkable," Roberts said as media squeezed into the small manager's office on the visitor's side at loanDepot Park. "This game has been around for a long time, and to do something that's never been done—he's one of one."

Statistician Sarah Langs ticked off Ohtani's accomplishments:

- He is the first player with a three-homer game to also steal multiple bases in that game.
- He is the first player since at least 1901 with at least five hits, multiple home runs, and multiple steals in the same game.
- He is the first leadoff hitter with a 10-RBI game. None of the previous 15 players who drove in 10 or more runs stole a base during the same game.
- He is the first player to hit a home run and steal a base in the same game 14 times in a single season, breaking the previous record of 13 by Rickey Henderson, in 1986.

"We all know we witnessed history today," Miguel Rojas said.

Asked during a postgame interview on MLB Network if he had been able to retrieve the 50-50 ball, Ohtani responded in English, "Not yet."

That would prove to be an understatement.

Ohtani's 50th home run ball left the field in seconds. The legal battle for the ball would go on for weeks, with two fans each claiming they had rightfully recovered the ball in the outfield seats at loanDepot Park.

A similar legal battle ensued after Barry Bonds' record-breaking 73rd home run ball, in 2001. That dispute was eventually settled in Solomon-like fashion—a judge ordered the men to sell the ball and split the proceeds. It went for $450,000 at auction.

Ohtani's 50-50 ball headed toward the same fate.

As the World Series was about to begin, in late October, Ohtani's 50-50 ball sold at auction for $4.392 million, with an agreement reached between the auction house and all parties claiming ownership. The auction price will be held in an account until the lawsuits are settled.

It was a record price for any piece of sports memorabilia, topping the $3 million paid for Mark McGwire's 70th home run ball from 1998—and just one of the many ways various parties had profited from the Shohei Ohtani phenomenon.

The most prominent beneficiaries, obviously, were the Dodgers. The marriage of their own powerful brand with Ohtani's was a massive success in its first year.

"You ask me, 'Has it lived up to expectations?' No—it's way beyond anything before. Way beyond," team president and CEO Stan Kasten said, the volume of his voice increasing on "way" and his arms gesturing toward the sky above Dodger Stadium.

"It's blown away any projections we could have had. Absolutely."

An executive in the NBA, NHL, and professional women's hockey, along with his decades of experience in MLB, Kasten said "it's almost never a factor" to consider the marketing or sales impact of signing a particular free agent.

"Because most players don't move the needle by themselves, especially in baseball," Kasten said. "In basketball, it could be a factor. You sign a LeBron. You sign a Shaq. You sign a Kobe. It changes your economics, as well as what your team does on the field. Not in baseball. It doesn't exist in baseball. No player moves the needle like that.

"Remember—we were already performing at the top of the business model for the sport. So how much extra could he provide? Turns out—way more than we thought."

The Dodgers drew just short of 4 million fans during the regular season in 2024, leading the major leagues as they have every year since the Guggenheim Group took over ownership in 2013.

There was little room for improvement there—but the Ohtani effect found a way.

"We have fewer no-shows than ever before," Kasten boasted.

Demand also spilled over into the secondary market, where tickets to Dodgers games were hot items.

The Ohtani effect worked on the road as well, where teams specifically advertising when the Dodgers—and Ohtani—would be coming to town.

"What we're seeing around the league…they are selling to Japanese sponsors that probably can't get into Dodger Stadium," Dodgers chief marketing officer Lon Rosen said. "So you see signage when he's up at bat. We did the same thing [at Dodger Stadium] when he was on the Angels…. There are agencies in Japan that are selling to companies at a different level than at Dodger Stadium."

At Dodger Stadium, sales at the team store were boosted by Ohtani's presence on the field—and the team's successful run in the postseason. Teams benefit at a different level from sales at team stores as compared to online sales or sales through MLB.

"Our merchandise sales have increased quite a bit," Rosen said. A quick look at all the No. 17 Dodgers jerseys in the stands on any given night provided the evidence.

Early in the year, the Dodgers seemed to announce a new sponsorship agreement with a Japanese company every other day. Rosen said the team added 12 Japanese sponsors in 2024.

"We were already at the top for the sport. We'll be significantly above that this year," Kasten said. "We had a unique thing here, which I don't think could have been replicated with any other team. It was the combination of our brand and our history, our legacy, our standing historically and contemporaneously with Shohei's worldwide appeal—and the drama of the runup to 'Who is going to sign him?' It was all of that built up to a unique result.

"He was a phenomenon unlike any other. This is baseball putting its best foot forward. And it had nothing to do with anything that we've done here. This is 'The Dodgers' and 'The Ohtani Phenomenon' together at their peaks. It's a great thing for baseball. It has really helped their business and their appeal internationally. That's not a benefit to us directly. It is indirectly. But it has been a great thing for baseball."

It certainly appears to have directly impacted the composition of the Dodgers' fan base.

"We have many more Japanese fans," Rosen said. "We don't have an exact figure. But a figure we were given a couple weeks ago—80 percent of Japanese people that visit Los Angeles wind up going through Dodger Stadium one way or another—whether they're attending a game, touring the stadium, or just stopping by and taking pictures. We see the impact on a daily basis."

The stadium tours became so popular in 2024—and thus lucrative—that the Dodgers began offering a full menu of options.

"We have, I think, a dozen different kinds of tours, including different language tours," Kasten said. "You can come early. You can come late and stay for BP. You can come even later and get a ticket for the game."

Ohtani himself certainly benefits from his popularity—so much so that he could afford to defer 97 percent of his 10-year contract and take only $2 million in annual salary.

Estimates are that Ohtani made at least $65 million in endorsements in 2024, with the possibility of that reaching $100 million with a World Series championship, a number that increased simply with his move from the Angels to the Dodgers. According to a *Forbes* magazine ranking, only NBA stars LeBron James and Giannis Antetokounmpo and soccer star Lionel Messi make more from endorsements than Ohtani who has deals with New Balance, BOSS, Porsche, Fanatics, Rapsodo, Seiko, Kosé, and Nishikawa, among others.

And he is loyal. Walking in and out of the Dodgers' clubhouse before and after games, home or road, Ohtani always wore some combination of BOSS and New Balance. When he needed to thank Ashley Kelly for helping him get his uniform number from Ashley's husband, Joe Kelly, he gave her a Porsche—and when he gave Dave Roberts a toy car as a joke after breaking his Dodgers "record" for home runs by a Japanese-born player, it was also a Porsche.

Like Kasten, Lon Rosen spent time working in the NBA and as an agent with elite athletes like Magic Johnson. But he has no comp for Ohtani.

"I believe he's set a new bar," Rosen said. "His popularity is different than any other athlete I've been around. I've visited Japan quite a bit, and he is by far the most popular athlete or personality in Japan, and I'm not sure who No. 2 is. He's got a whole country, and then he's captured so many people's imaginations here in this country, and really throughout the world. He performs so well on the field. He carries himself with such dignity. He's a special one.

"I've seen the great ones play—from Magic to Kobe to Tom Brady. His impact is up there, if not past it. I'm too young and it was before the boom of sports marketing, but I would say [Muhammad] Ali was probably a step above him. But Shohei, for a team sport player, I don't think there's ever been another like him."

The 6-for-6, 50-50 day in Miami propelled Ohtani like a rocket toward the finish line of the regular season.

Back home at Dodger Stadium the next night, Ohtani was given a standing ovation before his first at-bat, his teammates leaving the dugout and gathering in front to join the chorus. It was an "impromptu" choice for which Dave Roberts credited Clayton Kershaw.

"It was amazing," Ohtani said of the moment. "I'm just very grateful and thankful that, this being my first season with the Dodgers, I was able to experience this."

He struck out in that at-bat but had hits in his next three at-bats, including his 52nd home run of the season.

Starting with that historic game in Miami, Ohtani went 27-for-43 (.628) over the Dodgers' final 10 games. He had six home runs, six doubles, 20 RBIs, and 10 stolen bases.

"Knowing him...he's probably looking at 60-60," Dave Roberts said. "You never know with him."

As it turned out, Ohtani was just a rules decision away from a 60-steal season. In the penultimate game of the regular season, on September 28 at Coors Field, Ohtani stole two bases. A scoring change took one away.

In the fifth inning, Ohtani drew a leadoff walk. While Rockies starter Antonio Senzatela was pitching to Mookie Betts, Ohtani took off for second base and made it without a throw. But Senzatela was called for a balk.

By rule, Ohtani could not have been thrown out trying to advance on a balk, so he couldn't be awarded a stolen base for making it safely.

Ohtani finished the season with 59 stolen bases.

Ohtani's closing burst briefly raised the possibility of a Triple Crown season, something the National League hasn't seen since Joe Medwick in 1937.

He finished with 54 home runs and 130 RBIs, leading the National League in both categories. But he finished second to San Diego's Luis Arráez for the batting title, .310 to .314—a difference of just three hits.

But Ohtani's flair for the dramatic was second to none.

His 30th home run of the season was hit nearly out of Dodger Stadium. He had three hits and a home run on Japanese Heritage Night, two hits (including a home run) after Decoy stole the show on their bobblehead night. He homered in the All-Star Game and hit a walkoff grand slam to reach 40-40. And his epic 50-50 day in Miami will be remembered as one of the greatest individual moments in baseball history.

Before the curtain came down on Ohtani's first regular season with the Dodgers, he and Mookie Betts combined for another dramatic moment.

The Dodgers went into the ninth inning on September 22 trailing the Rockies, 5–4. A Sunday afternoon crowd of over 50,000 was watching the first-place Dodgers about to lose two of three to the last-place Rockies at home, bringing the second-place Padres (8–1 in their past nine games) to town for a three-game series just two games back and still very much alive in the NL West.

Rockies manager Bud Black gave the ball to young right-hander Seth Halvorsen to close out the game. Halvorsen fell behind Ohtani 2-and-1, then left a splitter up over the heart of the plate.

Ohtani did not miss, sending a 114.7-mph rocket 432 feet into the right-center field seats to tie the game. Showing more emotion than observers had become accustomed to seeing from him over the years—a theme down the stretch in 2024, his first taste of playoff race baseball—Ohtani pointed back at his teammates in the Dodgers' dugout as he started running the bases and could be seen yelling, "Let's go!"

It was Ohtani's fourth hit of the game, giving him a three-hit game, a four-hit game, and a six-hit game over his previous four games.

"He just doesn't seem human right now," Dave Roberts said.

The stadium got even louder three pitches later when Mookie Betts turned on a 100.6-mph fastball from Halvorsen, sending it into the left-field seats to complete the back-to-back and win the game.

The Dodgers spilled out of the dugout in celebration, very aware of what this meant in the NL West race.

"It was huge—especially when you're looking at the scoreboard and you see San Diego won," Betts said. "I didn't mean to look at it, but they won, and we needed to win a game there."

The dramatic turnaround was "enormous," Roberts said, citing a number of factors heading into the showdown series with the Padres, including their dominance over the Dodgers during the season (7–3 to that point) and the Dodgers' break-even play over their previous 12 games.

"To lose a series [to the Rockies], it would have been tough," Roberts said. "Just mentally feeling a little bit like you're on your heels."

Buoyed by the walkoff win, the Dodgers still lost the opener of the series to the Padres in shocking fashion. A game-ending triple play closed it out with Shohei Ohtani standing on deck.

"There's less than a 1 percent chance that Shohei doesn't come up to bat," Roberts said. "It's shocking.... That's the least likely outcome, obviously looking at how the game is played and how many triple plays are turned in a year."

According to statistician Sarah Langs, it was just the 28th game-ending triple play in MLB history. It was the fourth turned by a team that also clinched a postseason berth. But the Padres were the first to do both and they celebrated heartily, spilling out of the cramped visitors' clubhouse at Dodger Stadium and onto the field in front of the visitors' dugout long after the game was over.

The Dodgers had absorbed blow after blow all season long with player after player lost to injury. But they kept bouncing back. This series was no different.

With Ohtani scoring one run and driving in two more, the Dodgers beat the Padres 4–3 the next night. The following day, the Dodgers landed the knockout blow with a five-run seventh inning, beating the Padres 7–2 to clinch their 11th National League West division title in the past 12 years.

"They all feel sweet but I'll tell you, man, with what we've gone through this year, this feels a tick sweeter," Roberts said. "It was hard-fought. We earned it."

It was an RBI single by Ohtani in the seventh inning—one of his three hits on the day—that gave the Dodgers their first lead of the game.

"I'm really happy," Ohtani said through his interpreter, enjoying his first champagne celebration in MLB. "Today, I came to the stadium really wanting to clinch and I'm happy we did that today."

Roberts joked that Ohtani had been showered with so much champagne and beer "he's going to smell like a brewery for the next week."

"This is what Shohei signed up for," Roberts said. "This is what he wanted to be a part of. Shohei's just been remarkable this entire season."

Remarkable didn't seem to cover it. Ohtani's unprecedented 50-50 season included leading the National League in home runs (54), RBIs (130), runs scored (134), on-base percentage (.390), slugging percentage (.646), and OPS (1.036). His 411 total bases were the fifth-most in MLB since 1940. His 54 home runs and 99 extra-base hits set new franchise records.

Ohtani finished the season on a 12-game hitting streak during which he went 29-for-53, raising his batting average for the season 22 points in that time (from .288).

"I think the thing that I marvel at is the expectations that are put on him, that he puts on himself, and to still go out there every day and put on a show," Roberts said. "I can't imagine the pressure with all those expectations."

The Dodgers had their own expectations to meet in the postseason—and their nemesis, the San Diego Padres, would be the first hurdle.

Chapter 9

Yamamoto's Year

Kenta Maeda had eight seasons in the NPB under his belt—including two seasons in which he won the Eiji Sawamura Award as the top pitcher—when he made the jump to Major League Baseball, signing with the Los Angeles Dodgers in January 2016.

Maeda was a reliable part of the Dodgers' starting rotation for four seasons, going 47–35 with a 3.87 ERA and starting 103 regular-season games in that time.

The postseason was a different story for Maeda.

The Dodgers made the playoffs each of Maeda's four seasons, and he started three times during their run in 2016—once against the Washington Nationals in the National League Division Series and twice in the National League Championship Series the Dodgers lost to the Chicago Cubs. Each of the next three postseasons, Maeda was moved into the bullpen, a role he accepted but in which he was not happy.

During the 2019 NLDS—again against the Nationals—Maeda came out of the bullpen in four of the five games, twice at Dodger Stadium.

Sitting in the stands with the soldout crowd for one of those games was a 21-year-old Yoshinobu Yamamoto. Yamamoto also attended the American League wild-card game between the Tampa Bay Rays and Oakland A's, at the Oakland Coliseum. But it was watching Maeda pitch for the Dodgers that he later said inspired him and sparked the idea that he could also pitch in Major League Baseball someday.

"That game really made me feel strongly about wanting to come overseas to play in the big leagues," Yamamoto said four years later, at Dodger Stadium again after signing with the Dodgers.

Two years after his first visit to Los Angeles, Yamamoto won the first of three consecutive Pacific League MVP Awards and three consecutive Sawamura Awards. He was very much on the radar of major-league scouts. But it was unclear when he might be ready to make the jump to MLB.

"Evaluating talent over there, we're always hyper aware of the guys that have real tools and perform," said Galen Carr, the Dodgers vice president for player personnel who has a great deal of experience scouting in Japan. "But if a guy comes up at 21, 22, and just dominates—that's great. You're going to spend some time on him. But you have a limited amount of time. There's a lot of players over there, a lot of foreign players you have to see and cover. So if you're chewing up a lot of bandwidth on guys who aren't going to come out for another three or four years—that's fine. That's good history.

"We started watching him regularly two years before he came out. We'd seen him prior to that. We had a history with him. We just wouldn't bear down on him, see 15 to 20 starts a year. It just didn't make a ton of sense, because there was a lot of runway between when he comes over. At that point, maybe there's some changes that are made, maybe there's some fluctuation in performance, maybe your interest waxes or wanes. But the last couple years prior to him coming out, we were on him pretty hard."

What scouts like Carr saw was Yamamoto dominating hitters in the NPB. He threw two no-hitters (in 2022 and 2023) and won the pitching Triple Crown (leading in wins, strikeouts, and ERA) three years in a row.

He also fared well in international competition, pitching for Japan's gold medal–winning team at the 2020 Olympics and, alongside Shohei Ohtani and Shōta Imanaga, led Samurai Japan to the championship in the 2023 World Baseball Classic.

Carr liked what he saw.

"Raw stuff, for sure. This is a kid that would sit 95, 96 [mph]," Carr said after Yamamoto had debuted with the Dodgers. "He stays off the barrel really well with his split[-finger fastball]. And it was the compete in him on the mound. It was watching him before a game, the intentionality of his practice and focus. It really stood out. The athleticism, the ability to repeat that delivery and execute pitches consistently—it's elite no matter what ball you're throwing or what kind of mound you're throwing off of.

"So we felt that combination was a really good one and would project well over here. The size, the usage patterns, that's another thing to figure out. But we felt really strongly in the person and the stuff and the athleticism and coordination."

Yamamoto turned 25 years old in August 2023, meaning he would not be subject to the bonus limits that apply to international free agents who are under 25. Anticipating he would be posted following the 2023 season, a parade of top MLB executives made trips to Japan, including Giants president of baseball operations Farhan Zaidi, Yankees GM Brian Cashman, and Cubs president of baseball operations Jed Hoyer—as well as Andrew Friedman and Brandon Gomes of the Dodgers.

When the Orix Buffaloes officially posted Yamamoto in November 2023, he immediately shot to the top of the list of free-agent starting pitchers—a group that included Blake Snell coming off his second Cy Young Award.

Every MLB team with money to spend was interested in signing Yamamoto. The right-hander had meetings with the Yankees, Mets, Phillies, Giants, Red Sox, and Dodgers during the 45-day window allowed by the posting system.

The Mets took their bid a step further. Owner Steve Cohen and president of baseball operations David Stearns traveled to Japan to meet with Yamamoto and his family. Cohen and Stearns were willing to make Yamamoto the highest-paid pitcher in baseball history—before he even threw his first MLB pitch.

But so were the Dodgers, who had something else on their side—Shohei Ohtani. Yamamoto's teammate from Samurai Japan was involved in the Dodgers' pitch to the young right-hander.

"He was never really pushy about it, like, 'Hey, come to the Dodgers,'" Yamamoto said through an interpreter during an MLB Network interview after his decision. "He mentioned over and over again, 'Wherever you end up, I'm going to support you, I'm going to be rooting you on.'

"But at the same time, he was really open and receptive to any questions that I may have had in this whole entire process, so that really meant a lot."

As the battle for Yamamoto settled into a Dodgers vs. Mets affair, the perception ran through baseball circles that the Mets were making the better offer—but Yamamoto preferred Los Angeles over New York for a number of reasons, including geography, personal history, and the presence of Ohtani.

Friedman heard the chatter.

"Those things you hear a lot and I never know what to make of that," he said. "And I'm never going to get the real answer to any of that anyway, so I don't spend much time thinking about that."

In the span of two weeks, Friedman had committed over $1 billion in salaries to two Japanese stars—one proven at the MLB level, one unproven there.

"Teams are aggressive, right?" Dodgers GM Brandon Gomes said. "We wanted him and kept going back and forth. You get to a point where for Yama it's just, 'Okay, I want to be a Dodger, let's get this done.'"

Along with the Mets, the Dodgers had another challenge to overcome. For reasons no one can specify, an understanding had developed that Japanese stars coming to MLB would not want to sign with a team that already had a Japanese star. The Dodgers were "very" aware of this while pursuing both Ohtani and Yamamoto, Friedman said, and it was one of the reasons they wanted Ohtani to be part of the recruitment process.

"But it never made sense to me," Friedman said. "I was very aware of it, and through conversations with both I asked the question and the feedback from Shohei was, 'That would be great.' Now how much of that ties back to the success they had with Samurai Japan, playing together and winning it [the WBC in 2023] and the positive feelings that come from that, I don't know the answer to.

"But when I posed that question to Shohei, he was, 'That would be great. I really enjoyed him. He's really good.' And when I asked Yamamoto, he said, 'That would be incredible. I would love to play with Shohei.'"

But it was not the Dodgers' intention to corner the market on Japanese superstars by signing both Ohtani and Yamamoto.

"It was the opportunity," Dodgers team president Stan Kasten said. "This was a player [Yamamoto], if he had been there any year we would have been after him. It just so happened that it was coming up this year [the same year as Ohtani's free agency].

"Both things were unique opportunities. The fact that we were able to do both of them was good fortune. But we would have been interested in either one of them in any year."

At his introductory press conference at Dodger Stadium, Yamamoto made it clear playing with Ohtani was not "the sole reason" he signed with the Dodgers over the Mets.

"Even if he went somewhere else, I probably still would have ended up in L.A. as a Dodger," Yamamoto said.

But the pitcher acknowledged that Ohtani's uniquely constructed contract had signaled to him the franchise's desire to win.

"The fact that Shohei was doing that also signaled to me that it wasn't just the front office, it was also the players that are bought into this winning atmosphere as well," Yamamoto said.

The successful pairing of Ohtani and Yamamoto had reverberations in Japan the increased the Dodgers' already high profile there. It's not overstating things to say the Dodgers became Japan's franchise in 2024—potentially paving the way for future Japanese stars to go from NPB to L.A.

"I mean, that was a side benefit to this," Andrew Friedman said. "There are 125 million people in Japan and they are incredibly passionate about baseball. They are getting better and better at developing talent. Like, going over to Miyazaki in February of 2023 as Samurai Japan was coming together and starting their workouts before the WBC, the amount of arm talent in that camp was incredible.

"Part of this, and it's far down the road, is there could be a seven-year-old Shohei or Yoshinobu who is starting their Little League career in Japan and their favorite team is the Dodgers. Just that affinity and how that may pay dividends down the road when he becomes a free agent and we're his ideal choice, that has benefits as well.

"Making this a destination spot where the best Japanese players want to come play has a lot of benefit. Then obviously the geography, the layout of the city, the strong Japanese presence here, the proximity to Japan vis-à-vis other major-league cities, all play into that desire to be the destination spot where the best Japanese players in the world want to be."

"It depends on what that player is prioritizing," GM Brandon Gomes said of any advantage the Dodgers might have with

Japanese players now. "There are a lot of really good players. The NPB is getting more and more talented on both sides, on the position player side and there are a lot of really talented arms. I guess it remains to be seen. We certainly hope our presence in Japan, with the success of Shohei and Yama and assuming our being on TV quite frequently, is a benefit.

"But I think it's always going to go back to the individual player and what are they prioritizing once they're a free agent."

By signing Yamamoto to a 12-year, $325 million contract (plus a $50.6 million posting fee), the Dodgers made another acquisition as well—Yada Sensei.

Osamu Yada—known as Yada Sensei—is a "biomechanical guru" and personal trainer who worked with Yamamoto during his career in Japan. The pair drew attention for their unique training methods emphasizing yoga-like movements and eschewing weight training.

During his days scouting Yamamoto, Dodgers vice president of player personnel Galen Carr saw the unique regimen.

"My parents were hippies. They still meditate and stuff. I get that. There's a connection to the world and a spirituality that isn't commonplace," Carr said. "So even though we're in this industry and there's like-minded thinking in a lot of ways on a lot of different subjects, we as an organization went into that with an open mind. His belief that a lot of things are connected to each other that we don't really think about all the time—to me it made sense. Sort of a holistic sort of approach to development. I guess there's some spirituality tied up in that too.

"It was definitely different, kind of off-the-wall. In some ways, you're like, 'Hey we don't have this figured out, as far as developing pitchers and keeping them healthy.'... No one has really figured it out."

The Dodgers got their first up-close look at Yamamoto's workouts during spring training, when Yada Sensei supervised a bare-footed Yamamoto going through his stretches, balancing on blocks, tossing soccer balls of various sizes, and, most eye-catching, throwing javelins for long distances.

A number of Yamamoto's new pitching staff-mates tried throwing the javelins, and some—Walker Buehler and Tyler Glasnow, notably—even tried Yada Sensei's workouts. Listed at 5-foot-10, 176 pounds, Yamamoto was one of the smallest starting pitchers in the majors.

"I mean, obviously Shohei has been here for years, so you kind of understand the kind of player he is," said Buehler, a wiry 6-foot-2, 185 himself. "But Yamamoto, this being his first time over here, I'm curious and interested to watch him through the year and see kind of some of the different methods and training stuff that he does.

"I think it's interesting. I'm sure it'll be different to watch. Most American guys train pretty similarly and obviously there's stories and stuff about how he works. Interested to see how that all goes."

Yada Sensei gained one new disciple in Mookie Betts, who adopted some of the drills into his daily routine and stuck with it all through the 2024 season.

"It's not like I'm just trying it to try it," Betts said in spring training. "It took me two weeks of just watching, going and talking to some family, some friends, some people that mean a lot to me.

"If it's good enough for him [Yamamoto]—it's working for him. I've got nine years [left on his contract with the Dodgers]. I've got to be the best Mookie I can be for nine years. Why wouldn't I be open to something that I deem as something that will help me be the best I can be for the next nine years?"

Dodgers pitching coach Mark Prior said he was glad to see the openness with which Yamamoto's singular approach was greeted.

"Whether it's us, whether it's our training staff, or whether it's PD [player development], that's something that I think is rooted in the culture of our organization—intellectual curiosity," Prior said. "You want to know, 'Okay, why do you do these things? What makes it work for him?' Because if it can help one other guy, it's totally worth having.

"Sticking your head in the sand is not the way to go."

While Yamamoto went through the routines of spring training, much of the talk centered on how he would handle the greater workload of the major leagues. But it was something else that required him to make his first adjustments.

MLB teams are much more aggressive about looking for information that will allow their hitters to anticipate what pitch is coming next. In his first Cactus League games, Yamamoto was tipping his pitches. The Dodgers worked with him on making adjustments with the positioning of his hands during his windup, but Yamamoto didn't handle the change well. It affected his command.

Both may have been in play when Yamamoto made his major-league debut in Korea against the San Diego Padres.

The second of the two-game Seoul Series was a 15–11 Padres victory that featured 34 hits, 14 walks, three hit batters, three wild pitches, and two errors.

Yamamoto set the tone. The first four Padres reached base against him in the first inning. Nine batters eventually went to the plate and Yamamoto threw 43 pitches in the five-run first. His debut went no further.

"I can't point to any one reason. It sucked. A five-spot early," Dodgers catcher Will Smith said. "They were kind of on everything a little bit. We fell behind some. They just executed. They just moved the ball forward, found some holes, and got guys in."

Yamamoto emerged from his debut with a 45.00 ERA.

"That's just not who he is," Dodgers manager Dave Roberts said.

"I think he's still feeling his way through some delivery stuff," Andrew Friedman said. "Early on [in spring training], we saw exceptional execution, and his last few haven't been as good from an execution standpoint. It is a significant strength for him, and when that's off it's going to be tougher."

Nine days later, Yamamoto made his U.S. debut against the St. Louis Cardinals and looked much more like the pitcher the Dodgers thought they had signed. He held the Cardinals scoreless for five innings (though the Dodgers lost in extra innings).

Yamamoto built momentum from there. Over 11 starts after the debacle in Korea, he was 6–1 with a 2.67 ERA, 74 strikeouts in 64 innings, and a .225 batting average against.

"I think the thing I'm learning about Yoshinobu is, it's very business-like," Dave Roberts said. "It wasn't good in South Korea. And he just came back and went to work. Then he had a good one, and then he went back to work. So he's very methodical about his preparation. And I love that."

His first MLB win came after another five scoreless innings on a cold day at Wrigley Field on April 6. Yamamoto allowed just three hits and struck out eight.

"I didn't really think about it," he said of the criticism and concern that followed his poor debut. "The season is long. We have a long way to go. I just took it one game at a time and I focused on one game at a time."

By the time the Dodgers went to New York for a three-game series against the Yankees in early June, Yamamoto was ready for his coming-out performance.

The Dodgers-Yankees series June 7–9 was as big as a June series can get. It was a clash of historic rivals both at or near the top of the standings in their respective leagues. All three games would be televised nationally on one network or another, eyeballs drawn to the star power of two players in the midst of MVP seasons—New York's Aaron Judge and L.A.'s Shohei Ohtani—and the teams with the two best records in baseball.

But Yamamoto stole the spotlight in the first game.

He dominated the Yankees hitters from the start, allowing just two hits—a first-inning double to Judge and a second-inning single to Trent Grisham—over seven scoreless innings. Yamamoto retired 12 consecutive hitters at one point and struck out seven.

The game stayed scoreless into the 11th inning before Teoscar Hernández's two-run double gave the Dodgers the win.

"His best outing as a Dodger," Dave Roberts said of Yamamoto's performance. "You could just see it. He felt it. He knew we needed it. And it brought out the best in him. I can't say enough about his effort tonight."

It was an MLB-high seven innings for Yamamoto on another career-high 106 pitches. The playoff atmosphere at Yankee Stadium added life to his fastball. He averaged 97 mph against the Yankees, up from 95.3 mph over his first 12 MLB starts.

"I think that was just my mechanics working very well today," Yamamoto said of his increased velocity.

"I did know this matchup was going to draw a lot of attention compared to the other series. But just like I've been saying, I was just trying to do what I've been doing in other games."

Unfortunately, Yamamoto wouldn't be able to repeat the performance for a long time. For all their efforts to protect the right-hander in his first MLB season—he never started on fewer than five days' rest to replicate his schedule in Japan—they couldn't avoid an injury.

Yamamoto had thrown the 19 hardest pitches of his season and 13 sliders, the most he had used the troublesome pitch in an MLB start. Yamamoto had downplayed the slider during his NPB career because of concerns that it might lead to injury.

After reporting some soreness after the Yankees series, the Dodgers gave Yamamoto a full week of rest before his next start. But he lasted just two innings against the Royals on June 15 at Dodger Stadium and left the game with triceps tightness.

The triceps discomfort proved to be a symptom of a shoulder injury. An MRI revealed a strained rotator cuff, an injury the Dodgers would handle cautiously given their 12-year, $325 million investment in Yamamoto. He didn't pitch again until

September, time enough for just four starts before the postseason began.

"If he were signed to a one-, two-, three-year deal, maybe we would have been a little more aggressive with his rehab," Andrew Friedman said. "But the point was to err more on the side of caution and do what we could to build it up and be really strong, because part of what we thought led to the injury was just the added intensity of pitching at Yankee Stadium, and October is that and more. So being cautious now before putting him into that October environment, that we may or may not be correct on, but that was part of the calculation."

When he did return to the mound for the Dodgers, Yamamoto's results were uneven. He didn't allow an earned run in his first two starts but he also didn't get past four innings. In his third start back, the Rockies tagged him for four runs in just three innings.

With just one day left in the regular season, Yamamoto went back to the mound for his final start before the postseason. This time, he was more efficient and held the Rockies to two runs while finally stretching out to five innings.

"I think that was good enough," Yamamoto said. "Today, I started gaining back good feelings and what I usually have in the game."

Dave Roberts called it a "great tune-up for Yoshinobu."

"I thought the fastball was really good, had life to it," Roberts said after the start in Colorado. "I thought the command of it was really good. There were some near-misses. As the game went on, the splitter got better. The curveball was good."

The win in Colorado left Yamamoto with a 7–2 record and 3.00 ERA in 18 starts over his first MLB season.

"It was not a perfect season for me due to my injury, because I was away from the team," Yamamoto said, assessing his rookie year. "However, I learned a lot. I experienced great things and my teammates helped accumulate the wins, leading us into October. I really appreciate it and I'll do my best to contribute."

With just three healthy starters—Jack Flaherty, Walker Buehler, and Yamamoto—heading into the postseason, Dodgers manager Dave Roberts knew he would have to get quality outings from the trio. Confidence would not be a problem, Roberts said, despite Yamamoto's lack of experience in an MLB postseason.

"I think that he's seen enough Major League Baseball and has performed enough to know that he's at the top of the food chain as far as talent," Roberts said. "He's a very confident player. That's what I saw. I feel he's going to be the same thing. Again, he's very talented, very confident, and he's understanding what gets hitters out here."

Chapter 10

First Postseason

On the workout day before the start of the National League Division Series between the Dodgers and the San Diego Padres, Shohei Ohtani came into the interview room to meet the media and share his thoughts before finally making his postseason debut in MLB.

"Are you nervous at all for just playing in the postseason for the first time?" Jack Harris of the *Los Angeles Times* asked.

Without waiting for his interpreter, Will Ireton, to translate the question into Japanese, Ohtani responded with a single word: "Nope."

The confident response needed no translation and made for a nice clip to build promo ads around—especially when paired with video of his second at-bat in Game 1 against the Padres.

Things had not started well for the Dodgers. They gave the ball to Yoshinobu Yamamoto in Game 1, despite his complete lack of experience in postseason play and the limited buildup he had managed in September after returning from a strained rotator cuff.

It looked like a bad choice when Yamamoto gave up three runs in the first inning, including two on a home run by Manny Machado. It was a poor start that awakened memories not only of Yamamoto's unsuccessful debut against the Padres in South Korea but also the ghosts of the 2023 NLDS against the Arizona Diamondbacks, when poor efforts from their starting pitchers doomed the Dodgers.

"I mean, you could almost feel it in the stadium," Dodgers third baseman Max Muncy said of the fear that spread among the sold-out crowd. "Then thankfully we have a guy whose name is Shohei Ohtani and he injected an absolute lightning bolt into the stadium. From then on, it was 'Alright, we've got this. This is not the same as years past. We're good.'"

Ohtani came up with two on and two out in the second inning. Ahead in the count 2-and-0 against Padres starter Dylan Cease, Ohtani got a fastball inside and fouled it off his left knee.

He took a moment before settling back in the batter's box. When Cease followed with a fastball at the top of the strike zone, Ohtani destroyed it, lining it at 111.8 mph into the right-field pavilion seats for a three-run, game-tying home run. Firing his bat away with a two-handed toss, Ohtani yelled, "Let's go!" toward his teammates in the dugout, an early signal that this year's team had more fight in it than the 2022 and 2023 versions.

But Yamamoto did not have it. He gave up two more runs to put the Dodgers down again. He lasted just three innings.

It was the 15th time in Dodgers history that they had fallen behind by three runs or more after the first inning of a postseason game. It was the first time they would come back to win.

"We need to fight. And that's what we did tonight," Dodgers manager Dave Roberts said after the game, establishing a theme that would persist throughout their postseason run. "We didn't get an ideal start. But guys in the 'pen picked us up and the offense was relentless with their at-bats."

Five Dodgers relievers combined for six scoreless innings, allowing just two hits after Yamamoto left the mound.

While the relievers held the fort, the offense rode to the rescue. A three-run fourth inning featuring a broken-bat single by Ohtani and a two-out, two-run single by Teoscar Hernández gave the Dodgers their first lead in a postseason game since Game 4 of the 2022 NLDS, against the Padres.

An unearned run gave them a little cushion and the relievers put away a 7–5 Game 1 victory.

"They jumped on us, punched us in the mouth," Dodgers catcher Will Smith said. "We knew we weren't out of it. Just gotta keep fighting."

There was more punching to come.

The Padres roared back in Game 2, hitting six home runs (a record for a road team in a postseason game) in a 10–2 victory that featured taunting and trolling by Padres outfielders Jurickson Profar and Fernando Tatís Jr. and poor behavior by the Dodgers' fans surrounding them in the rowdy pavilion seats.

"It's a show. It's *MLB: The Show*," Tatís said of the interaction between he and Profar and the Dodgers fans. "We were giving them a show."

The show started in the first inning when Mookie Betts—hitless in 22 consecutive postseason at-bats by the end of Game 2—drove a fly ball into the left-field corner. Betts went into his home run trot, relieved that his postseason slump was over. The stadium sound system started the home run fanfare.

One problem—Profar had reached into the stands and caught the fly ball, taking it away from the fans and taunting them as he strutted away with the ball in his glove.

"I don't know really what to say about it," said Betts after his postseason slump had grown by four more hitless at-bats. "I'm giving my best, doing my best. Obviously it's not good enough right now."

Starter Jack Flaherty was not good enough either. He allowed four runs in 5⅓ innings and got into a verbal battle with Padres third baseman Manny Machado after Flaherty hit Tatís with a pitch in the sixth inning.

"They didn't like the pitch to Tatís," Flaherty said. "Look, I missed in the first inning and I threw the ball over the middle [leading to the first of Tatís' two home runs]. I wasn't going to miss over the plate again."

Flaherty was also triggered when Machado threw a ball being used to warm up between innings at the Dodgers' dugout, bouncing it off the netting in front of Dodgers manager Dave Roberts. Roberts called it "unsettling" and "pretty disrespectful," fueling the media fires on the off day following Game 2.

Far more unsettling was the unruly behavior of the Dodgers fans. Responding to more taunting from Profar, a ball was thrown from the left-field pavilion toward the outfielder, prompting a 12-minute delay before the bottom of the seventh inning. The umpiring crew called for more security in the outfield, the unrest spreading to the right-field pavilion when Tatís started dancing and making gestures at the fans to wipe away their tears.

"Dodger fans, they were just not happy," Tatís said later. "They're losing the game, obviously, and just a lot of back and forth."

The Dodgers put up little fight, managing just one run on three hits in seven innings against Padres right-hander Yu Darvish.

"We were shit," Muncy summarized after the game.

They were also not at full strength—a season-long theme. Freddie Freeman had badly sprained his ankle on September 26. He sat out the rest of the regular season, acknowledging that the training staff had told him it was "a four-to-six-week thing."

Freeman, and the Dodgers, didn't have four to six weeks. He went through hours of daily treatment, took pain-killing injections, and "willed himself into the lineup," Dave Roberts said. But he left Game 2 after five innings when the ankle became too painful to play on, and he would miss three games in the NLDS and NLCS against the Padres and the New York Mets, respectively.

What didn't become public until later—revealed by his father—was that Freeman also played with an intercostal injury, involving his ribs, that he suffered the day before the start of the NLDS. The combination of injuries made Freeman a non-factor against the Padres and Mets (7-for-32 with no extra-base hits).

The Dodgers sent Walker Buehler to the mound for Game 3 in San Diego, hoping his pedigree as a big-game pitcher would supersede his miserable season—1–6 with a 5.38 ERA after returning from a second Tommy John surgery.

"It's kind of the only thing I care about," Buehler said when asked about his reputation for rising to the moment.

He couldn't rise above the poor defense around him in Game 3.

Mookie Betts' first-inning home run—Jurickson Profar couldn't reach that one—sent Buehler to the mound with a 1–0 lead in the second inning. Things got ugly from there.

Manny Machado led off with a single. Jackson Merrill hit a hard ground ball to Freddie Freeman's right. Freeman made the stop and tried to throw from his knees to second base. The ball hit Machado in the back of the shoulder.

The Dodgers' pleas for an interference call on Machado went unheeded. He was within his right as a baserunner to "create his own baseline until there's an actual attempted play on him," the rulebook states.

"That's the highest IQ in baseball," Tatís said of his teammate. "When you see plays like that.… that's why Manny's Manny."

Miguel Rojas made things worse for the Dodgers when he fielded Xander Bogaerts' slow ground ball near second base and tried to turn a double play on his own, rather than flip to second baseman Gavin Lux for the force out. He didn't get either out and a run scored on the play.

"That play has happened to me in my career a bunch of times and more times than not—I think 99 percent—today was the only time that I haven't gotten the runner at least at second base," said Rojas, who was playing with an adductor tear that would knock him off the roster for the NLCS. "But at the end of the day, you rethink about it and revisit the play and all we needed was one out. I didn't know that the whole thing was going to happen after, obviously, but getting one out there probably was the best option, and I made a bad decision."

"The whole thing" that happened was a six-run inning. David Peralta drove in two with a double after Rojas' misplay. One pitch from escaping the nightmare inning, Buehler gave up a two-run homer to Tatís on an 0-and-2 fastball.

When Buehler finally retired the side, he took out his frustrations in the Dodgers' dugout, slamming his glove down, firing a cooler into the bench, and tossing assorted items around in anger.

Teoscar Hernández made it a one-run game with a third-inning grand slam, and the Dodgers allowed just two hits after the wayward second inning. But the 6–5 Padres victory put the Dodgers down two games to one in the best-of-five NLDS, one loss away from a third consecutive first-round playoff exit.

"What's done is done now," Ohtani said. "So at this point, it's really very simple…win two games."

Betts narrowed the focus even more.

"We can't look at the mountain. We have to just look at the task at hand, and that's one pitch at a time," he said. "It's going to be obviously a lot more pressure. Each at-bat is going to matter exponentially more. So figure out a way to get it done."

The Dodgers would have to figure it out without a starting pitcher.

With injuries having taken Tyler Glasnow, Gavin Stone, and Clayton Kershaw out of the postseason picture, the Dodgers went into October with only three starting pitchers—Flaherty, Yamamoto, and Buehler. The math was simple—three wasn't enough. They would have to resort to a "bullpen game"—deploying a relay team of relievers to cover nine innings—at least once in each playoff round for as long as they stayed alive.

The starting pitching issues that plagued them all season forced the Dodgers to lean heavily on their bullpen throughout the 2024 season, preparing them for this. They came through in Game 4, as eight relievers stitched together nine shutout innings and the Dodgers staved off elimination with an 8–0 shutout.

"I think the bullpen were the players of the game tonight," Kiké Hernández said accurately. It was only the second postseason shutout featuring at least eight pitchers.

"This isn't our first bullpen game," said Anthony Banda, the second of those eight pitchers. "It's understanding that the bullpen is a very important piece of this ballclub and there's a reason for that. I don't think anybody deviated from what we've done in the regular season. I think everyone just went and laid it all out there because we knew what was at stake.

"We understood the assignment and we just continued to pass that baton on and understand we have that trust in the person coming in behind us."

Back at Dodger Stadium for a winner-take-all Game 5, the Dodgers sent Yamamoto back to the mound, hoping for better results than he gave them in Game 1. The numbers were not on their side. The Padres seemed to have Yamamoto's number: in two regular-season starts and Game 1 of the NLDS, they had scored 13 runs in nine innings against him.

But on this night, Yamamoto was, in teammate's Kiké Hernández's words, "filthy."

He gave up just two hits and a walk in five scoreless innings, starting the Dodgers on their way to a second consecutive shutout victory. Home runs by Kiké Hernández and Teoscar Hernández gave the Dodgers a 2–0 victory and punched their ticket to the National League Championship Series against the Mets.

"He was wearing what he did in the first one. He was emotional about it—felt like he didn't do his job," Dodgers pitching coach Mark Prior said of Yamamoto. "Everybody was there to pump him up and support him. That happens. Even the best names in the game have had tough times in the playoffs."

But Yamamoto and the bullpen combined to help the Dodgers break out of "a little bit of a DS funk," as Andrew Friedman dared to describe the consecutive first-round failures. Fans and critics who had questioned whether Dave Roberts would keep his job after a third were now praising his brilliant handling of the Dodgers' compromised pitching staff.

"We have such a fan base and we love that," Friedman said after the Game 5 victory. "The expectations are super high. We love that as well. And whenever we fall short of that, there's a lot of blame to go around and a lot of disappointed people. We would much rather that than people not caring.

"The theater of October baseball is all outcome-based. If you have a good outcome, positive things are said and written. If you have a bad outcome, really bad things are said and written."

The theater was being enjoyed by the largest viewing audiences in years. In Japan, Game 5 of the NLDS—featuring the starting pitching matchup of Yu Darvish and Yoshinobu Yamamoto, as well as Shohei Ohtani—was the most watched MLB postseason game ever in Japan, despite starting at 9:00 AM there.

Much was still to be written about the Dodgers' postseason. But the truth was that in facing down a Padres team that was nearly as talented, played with an irritating swagger, and knew how to get under their skin, the Dodgers had just beaten the best team they would face in October. Everyone felt it—whether they dared give voice to it or not.

"I'll just pick one player but it was more than one," Dodgers controlling owner Mark Walter would say later. "San Diego is a very good team. Say whatever you want to say about the rivalry—they're a very, very good team. After we beat them, [Clayton] Kershaw came over and said to me, 'We're going to the World Series.'"

Dave Roberts took it a step further, saying in November of the NLDS with the Padres, "That was the World Series."

Of course, there was still an NLCS to be played against a Mets team that wanted to think it fit the profile of recent October overachievers that had found their stride in midseason and caught lightning in a bottle during the postseason.

The Mets were going nowhere with a 28–37 record on June 12, pilloried as another waste of Steve Cohen's millions. Then something happened—McDonald's marketing character Grimace threw out a ceremonial first pitch as part of a promotion at Citi Field. The Mets took off. Their 61–36 record from that day to the end of the season was the best in baseball, better even than the Dodgers'. They survived a plus-one-day doubleheader to claim the NL's last postseason berth and kept going all the way to the NLCS.

The magic drained away against the Dodgers.

With Jack Flaherty handling the first seven innings, the Dodgers spun a third consecutive shutout, holding the Mets to just three hits in a 9–0 Game 1 rollover.

The Dodgers had not given up a run since those defensive breakdowns led to a six-run belch in the second inning of Game 3 in the NLDS. Thirty-three consecutive scoreless innings since then tied the longest streak in postseason history. (The Baltimore Orioles shut out the Dodgers for 33 consecutive innings during the 1966 World Series.)

"It was just a pitching clinic," Roberts said specifically of Flaherty's effort in Game 1.

Ohtani was on base three times in the win, scored two runs, and drove in one with a single.

"I think after an intense series like the last one where you play with a lot of energy, we were aware that you can definitely fall into a little lull and come out flat," Tommy Edman said. "So we really made it a priority to come out with that energy and really take it to them, and we did a great job of that in the first few innings."

The Mets stole that formula in Game 2.

The Dodgers' second go-round with a bullpen game didn't go as well as the first. Francisco Lindor led off the game with a home run against Ryan Brasier, ending the Dodgers' run of scoreless innings, and the Mets added five runs in the second inning. With Alex Vesia off the NLCS roster thanks to an injury to his oblique and Daniel Hudson nursing a sore knee, the Dodgers' bullpen was short-handed. Dave Roberts had to try and get innings out of right-hander Landon Knack. But the rookie gave up a grand slam to Mark Vientos in the five-run second inning.

The Dodgers never recovered from that rough start and the NLCS was even after a 7–3 Mets victory in Game 2.

"It's all great when it works well and guys are throwing up zeros," Roberts said of the bullpen game strategy getting knocked off the rails.

Ohtani was 0-for-3 in Game 2, though he did walk twice. But his first postseason experience had slipped into a very odd pattern. Through five games of the NLDS and the first two of the NLCS, Ohtani was a robust 6-for-8 with runners on base—but 0-for-19 when he came up with the bases empty.

"I think Shohei will be fine," Mookie Betts said after Game 2, greeting the question about Ohtani's splits with bemusement and disdain.

But Ohtani was just 5-for-24 with 12 strikeouts since his home run and single against the Padres in Game 1 of the NLDS.

"What I really focus on is how I feel at the plate," Ohtani said before Game 3. "If I'm feeling good and the results aren't there, then I'm not too concerned, because there's luck involved.

"Now, if there's a situation where I don't feel good at the plate and I'm not doing well, or it's not leading to good results, then it's something that I look into to make sure physically, mechanically, making sure that that's all fine-tuned."

Asked how he felt at that point, he offered only "okay" by way of assessment. What he might have been keeping to himself, though, was a realization of how difficult postseason at-bats are when teams are game planning and working matchups to stop you.

Ohtani was 0-for-13 with nine strikeouts against three specific pitchers. In the NLDS, the Padres deployed ace lefty reliever Tanner Scott four times against Ohtani. He struck out all four times. Facing his "childhood hero" Yu Darvish twice in that series, Ohtani was 0-for-6 with three strikeouts. And the Mets started left-hander Sean Manaea—a pitcher who throws from a unique arm angle—in Game 2 of the NLCS. Ohtani was 0-for-3 with two strikeouts against him.

Ohtani was reminded of the postseason struggles of other great players—Betts himself had started the 2024 postseason in an 0-for-22 slump. On the other side of the bracket, AL MVP Aaron Judge was struggling as well. Legends including Barry Bonds and Alex Rodriguez had also had underachieving Octobers.

"It's hard for me to say if I'm at the same standard as the players you mentioned," Ohtani said. "This is my first experience in the postseason, so I can't really rely on the experiences or my reflection on the past. But what I do know is that we've been playing against good teams, better teams, with their best pitchers. So being able to get base hits, put up results isn't as easy maybe as it could be."

It was easy in Game 3. The Dodgers took advantage of poor Mets defense for an early 2–0 lead, then broke it open late with home runs from Kiké Hernández, Max Muncy, and Ohtani himself.

Ohtani's eighth-inning blast was his only hit of the game and came—of course—with two runners on. Hit 115.9 mph off the bat, it was such a towering drive that the umpires went to a replay review to make sure it left the field in fair territory.

"I don't know how you ever overturn it," Muncy said. "That ball was 100 feet over the foul pole. The foul pole is not tall enough for that one."

Ohtani led off Game 4 with another home run, a 117.8-mph missile into the New York bullpen on the second pitch of the game from Mets starter José Quintana—Ohtani's first hit of the postseason without a runner on base.

"I can't even hit the ball that hard with an aluminum bat, and Shohei is doing it with [a wood bat]," Freddie Freeman marveled.

The Dodgers never trailed in a 10–2 runaway that put them in control of the best-of-seven series. Ohtani walked three times in the game and scored four of the Dodgers' 10 runs.

"He changes the game every time he steps in the box," Betts said of Ohtani. "He's like a cheat code."

Betts was doing alright for himself. He had four hits and drove in four runs in the Game 4 victory.

In fact, the Dodgers' lineup was wearing the Mets out from top to bottom. They drew 31 walks in the first four games of the NLCS, the most for any four-game span in any postseason. Twelve of those walks had turned into runs—the Mets had scored a total of just nine runs in the first four games.

Muncy personified the "no-chase" approach. He reached base in 12 consecutive plate appearances—eight walks, two singles, and two home runs. That was a record for a single postseason, and tied Reggie Jackson for the overall postseason record. (Jackson's streak of 12 started in the 1977 World Series and stretched into the 1978 postseason.)

"You've got to give them credit, because that's a really good lineup and they can do a lot of different things," Mets manager Carlos Mendoza said after Game 4. "This is a team that controls the strike zone as well as anybody in the league. Not only do they do that, but when they force you in the zone, they can do some damage. And they've done that. They did it again today."

They only had to do it once more in order to advance to the World Series. Jack Flaherty made that impossible.

Flaherty had dominated the Mets with seven scoreless innings in Game 1 but he couldn't approach that in Game 5. He gave up eight runs in three innings and the Dodgers never recovered, losing 12–6 and taking a three-games-to-two advantage back to Los Angeles.

Flaherty's fastball velocity was down. He averaged 91.2 mph on his 26 four-seamers. And his command was off. He couldn't find the strike zone consistently, and the Mets were waiting when he did. They hit nine balls with exit velocities of 98 mph or higher in Flaherty's three innings.

But the Dodgers' offense kept rolling. Rookie outfielder Andy Pages hit two home runs and Mookie Betts another one—positive signs for the push to close out the series at home.

They would need that offense, because Game 6 would be yet another bullpen game.

It was far from flawless but it didn't need to be. The offense put up eight runs or more for the fourth time in the six games and the Dodgers fulfilled their annual "World Series or Bust" expectations with a 10–5 win, closing out the Mets.

Tommy Edman drove in four runs with a two-run double and a two-run home run and claimed the NLCS MVP trophy. His 11 RBIs in the six games against the Mets matched the Dodgers' postseason record set by Corey Seager during their seven-game NLCS victory over the Atlanta Braves, in 2020.

Will Smith also homered in the Game 6 victory and Ohtani reached base three times on two singles and a walk.

The 46 runs the Dodgers scored against the Mets in the NLCS were a franchise record for any postseason series and a National League record for the LCS.

And it set up a dream matchup for MLB in the World Series—Dodgers vs. Yankees, two historic franchises with star power to burn.

"As a fan of baseball, how could you not be excited about this?" Max Muncy said in the celebratory clubhouse after Game 6. "You're talking about two of the biggest franchises. The biggest stars in the sport. You've got Freddie, Mookie, Shohei. On the other side, you've got Aaron Judge, Giancarlo Stanton, Juan Soto, Gerrit Cole. The game's biggest stars on the biggest stage—how can you not be excited about this as a fan?

"Come on, man. It's Dodgers-Yankees—come on!"

Chapter 11

World Series

The Dodgers and Yankees have history. Lots of it.

The former New York neighbors, now bi-coastal powers, met in the World Series for the 12th time in 2024—the most frequent World Series pairing of all—but the first time since 1981.

For Shohei Ohtani, it was the fulfillment of a quest that began when he signed with the Dodgers in December 2023.

"I'm so happy we've been able to take him from never going to the playoffs to now going to the World Series," team owner Mark Walter said while watching Ohtani celebrate with his teammates following the NLCS clincher.

"It's incredible," Dodgers president of baseball operations Andrew Friedman said. "The fact that this is the first October Shohei got to participate in, that our Dodger fans get to see him up close and personal in the playoffs, fans all over the world having this opportunity, I think is incredibly special.

"It's exactly what we talked about when we met with him in December, and for this to come to fruition in Year One and the ultimate goal this close in sight, I think it's really special for everyone."

It's nothing less than what is expected of the Dodgers every year, Max Muncy reminded everyone. But they had not been to the World Series since the "bubble" postseason of 2020.

"Every single team when they get to spring training, they say, 'Hey, our goal is to win the World Series this year,'" Muncy said. "We're one of the few teams where that's a realistic goal—every single year. There's a lot of pressure. There's a lot of expectations. Especially this year when you talk about some of the names we added. It definitely weighed heavily all year long."

Ohtani seemed to bear that weight easily. After defeating the New York Mets in the NLCS, his satisfaction was obvious, the victories validating his decision to leave Anaheim for Los Angeles and sign a contract featuring an unprecedented amount of deferred payment.

"I finally arrived at this stage," he said through his interpreter. "The goal was to get this far. And I also pictured myself getting this far with the contract that I've signed. And again, just being able to play on this kind of stage with the team effort and all the games were really hard. But I'm just glad that we're at this stage right now."

And what a stage it was—an MLB marketing-dream matchup of blue-blood franchises featuring some of the biggest stars in the game, all with their eyes on a championship.

"The juggernauts are here now," Yankees DH Giancarlo Stanton proclaimed.

The two World Series teams had much in common beyond their stars, payrolls, and expectations. Both teams relied on a combination of power and patience to muscle their way past teams. During the regular season, they had the two lowest chase rates in MLB, were second and third in runs scored, first and fourth in slugging percentage, first and third in home runs. The Yankees had one clear advantage—an ace-level starter in Gerrit Cole.

They sent him to the mound in Game 1 and got an ace-like performance. Cole retired 13 of the first 14 Dodgers. The lone hit was a surprise—a triple by Freddie Freeman.

The Dodgers closed out the Mets in Game 6 of the NLCS without playing Freeman, giving him a full week off for his sprained ankle to heal. It also gave Freeman a week to spend obsessing over adjustments to his swing that he insisted had nothing to do with his ankle injury. The triple was his first extra-base hit since he suffered that injury on September 26.

Jack Flaherty bounced back from his poor start in Game 5 of the NLCS, matching zeros with Cole into the fifth inning. But he gave up a leadoff single to Juan Soto in the sixth, and two batters later Stanton golfed a low breaking ball 412 feet down the left-field line for a two-run home run.

That 2–1 lead seemed to be in good hands with Cole. But Yankees manager Aaron Boone pulled Cole as soon as he gave up a leadoff single to Teoscar Hernández in the seventh, despite Cole having thrown only a manageable 88 pitches.

Nothing came of that, but the Dodgers tied the game in the eighth inning. Ohtani lined a double off the right-field wall, just a couple feet from being a home run, then went to third when the Yankees misplayed the relay throw. He scored the tying run easily on a sacrifice fly by Mookie Betts.

The game went into extra innings tied until the Yankees pushed across a run in the 10th inning.

In the bottom of the inning, a walk and an infield single put runners on for Ohtani with one out. Boone chose to bring in Nestor Cortés, a left-hander who had spent the season in the Yankees' starting rotation but hadn't pitched in a game since a mid-September flexor tendon injury.

"Just taking the left-on-left matchup there. No, I didn't deliberate long," Boone said later. "The reality is he's been throwing the ball really well the last few weeks as he's gotten ready for this."

Ohtani swung at the first pitch from Cortes, slicing a fly ball down the left-field line. Yankees left fielder Alex Verdugo gave chase and made a spectacular catch, tumbling into the stands. As a result of the dead ball, the baserunners—Tommy Edman at first, Chris Taylor at second—were each awarded a base, leaving first base open.

With two outs, Boone opted to intentionally walk Betts and try another left-on-left matchup—Cortés vs. Freeman.

Cortés started him off with an inside fastball—exactly the pitch Freeman said he was looking for. He lined it into the right-field pavilion for the first walkoff grand slam in World Series history.

Dodger Stadium exploded—and Freeman briefly lost his mind.

The homer was a no-doubter and Freeman raised his bat to the sky as he started up the first-base line before dropping it dramatically. With his teammates spilling onto the field, Freeman said he "blacked out" and was "just kind of floating." All he could remember was screaming as he rounded the bases, flexing toward the Dodgers' bullpen between second and third base.

After he crossed home plate, Freeman spotted his father, Fred, in the seats behind it. The two have an uncommon bond, forged through the tragedy of Freddie's mother's death when he was just 10 years old.

Forgotten were the sprained ankle and rib injury. Freeman charged toward the screen behind home plate where his father met him.

"He's been throwing me batting practice since I can remember," Freeman said. "My swing is because of him. My approach is because of him. I am who I am because of him.

"It was kind of spur of the moment. I saw him hugging a lot of people back there.... I just wanted to share that with him, because he's been there. He's been through a lot in his life, too, and just to have a moment like that—I just wanted to be a part of that with him in that moment.

"If he didn't love the game of baseball, I wouldn't be here playing this game. So that's Fred Freeman's moment right there."

It was bigger than that, though. It was a Kirk Gibson moment for a fan base that had been waiting for one since 1988.

"I'm probably one of, like, two people in here that was alive when that happened," 37-year-old reliever Daniel Hudson said. "It was almost the same situation, obviously. Bottom of the ninth, Game 1 of the World Series, a lefty comes up and absolutely nukes one. [Freeman's home run came in the 10th.] The comparisons between the two are just really freaking cool."

There was one difference that was important to Freeman.

"I played the whole game, though," he said.

Gibson's iconic home run came in a pinch-hit appearance, his only at-bat in the 1988 World Series due to leg injuries.

"When you're five years old with your two older brothers and you're playing Wiffle ball in the backyard, those are the scenarios you dream about—two outs, bases loaded in a World Series game," Freeman said. "For it to actually happen and get a home run and walk it off to give us a 1–0 lead [in the Series]—that's as good as it gets right there."

Dodger Stadium was still buzzing as another soldout crowd arrived for Game 2. They left in a much different mood.

The Dodgers gave them nothing to worry about for most of the game. Yoshinobu Yamamoto turned in another outstanding start. He allowed just one hit (a solo home run by Juan Soto) over six innings, retiring 11 batters in a row after that hit. Yankees slugger Aaron Judge had been neutered by Dodgers pitchers, going 1-for-9 with six strikeouts in the first two games of the World Series (after going 5-for-31 with 13 strikeouts in the Yankees' first two playoff series).

The Dodgers got home runs from Tommy Edman, Teoscar Hernández, and a rejuvenated Freeman on their way to a 4–2 victory. But the mood darkened in the seventh inning.

After drawing a one-out walk, Shohei Ohtani took off trying to steal second. He was thrown out by Yankees catcher Austin Wells. But Ohtani has a unique sliding motion, adopted to protect his pitching arm from danger. This time, he jammed his left arm into the ground, popping his shoulder out of its socket. He laid on the ground for some time in obvious pain, then left the field with a trainer, holding his left arm carefully against his side.

"Not only the dugout, but the whole stadium went silent," Teoscar Hernández said.

The Dodgers tried to minimize the injury afterward, saying the diagnosis was a subluxation—a partial dislocation—of the shoulder joint. Dodgers manager Dave Roberts pointed out that Ohtani's range of motion was good in postgame tests and that his strength in his left arm was "great." It was enough to be "encouraged," Roberts said.

"Obviously, it would be a huge hole," Kiké Hernández said of the possibility of playing on without Ohtani. "But if there's something about this team, guys are going to find ways to step up. We played some games without Freddie in the lineup, without Mookie, and we've won those games.

"We're hoping we don't play any games without Sho. But if we do, I'm sure we'll find somebody to step up for him."

Betts said he was "really confident" the Dodgers could still win without Ohtani, especially having built a two-game lead in the best-of-seven Series.

"We can take care of business, for sure," Betts said. "I believe in us all."

With that, the Dodgers packed up and headed for New York. Ohtani would stay behind and undergo an MRI on his shoulder before joining a second charter flight for family members the next day.

On the way to the airport, though, Ohtani's teammates got a text from him via the players-only group chat.

"Nice game, guys," he texted in English. "Last time, Bellinger's shoulder was dislocated. This time, my shoulder was dislocated. This is a good sign for a world champion."

Ohtani was referring to the Dodgers' most recent World Series victory, in 2020. Center fielder Cody Bellinger dislocated his right shoulder while celebrating a home run in Game 7 of the NLCS. He played through the World Series with the injury—though he went only 3-for-22 (albeit with a home run)—and later underwent surgery.

"He [Ohtani] texted the whole team as we were on our way to the airport and said he was going to be fine and that's it," Max Muncy said. "He said he was going to play, so we all put it to the side at that moment."

Ohtani would play. But he was not fine. When he did reach base in Game 3, he ran holding his left arm tight to his chest.

It didn't matter. The Dodgers were clearly the better team in this matchup.

Freddie Freeman hit a two-run home run in the first inning and Walker Buehler held the Yankees scoreless for five innings en route to a 4–2 Dodgers victory and a three-games-to-none lead in the Series.

"Just based off what he's done the last three games—we obviously have to find a way to win one more game, but let's say we win one more game at some point—I expect Freddie to never pay for a meal ever again in L.A.," Kiké Hernández said.

Freeman did it again in the first inning of Game 4—another two-run home run. The blast set two World Series records, making Freeman the first player to homer in each of the first four games of a World Series. Combined with home runs in the last two games of the 2021 World Series when he was with Atlanta, he also set the Series record for consecutive games with a home run (six).

But the Yankees finally got their own power game going. Anthony Volpe hit a grand slam and Gleyber Torres and Austin Wells also hit home runs in an 11–4 victory that prevented the first World Series sweep since 2012.

Game 5 was a rematch of the starting pitchers from the Series opener—Gerrit Cole and Jack Flaherty. Flaherty was not up to the moment.

He gave up back-to-back home runs in the first inning, to Aaron Judge and Jazz Chisholm Jr., and four runs while facing just nine batters and retiring only four before Dave Roberts pulled him from the game and essentially kicked into motion yet another bullpen game.

The Yankees made it a 5–0 lead after Giancarlo Stanton's solo home run in the third inning, and the Series seemed headed back to California. But the Yankees had gone as far as they could with a team that hit home runs by the bushel but did nearly everything else a baseball team is supposed to do poorly.

The decisive inning of the Series—and probably the worst defensive inning in World Series history—pulled the rug out from under Cole in the fifth inning.

Kiké Hernández led off the inning with a clean single but Tommy Edman hit a routine line drive right at Judge in center field. He dropped it, flubbed in inexplicable fashion, for an error.

Will Smith hit a ground ball to Anthony Volpe at shortstop and Volpe had the lead runner at third base. But he threw into the dirt and everyone was safe, loading the bases for the Dodgers with no outs.

Cole struck out Lux and Ohtani and seemed set to escape harm when he got Mookie Betts to dribble a ball to first baseman Anthony Rizzo. But Cole failed to cover first base and Rizzo was too slow to beat a hustling Betts to the bag. A run scored and the mood darkened at Yankee Stadium.

Freeman stroked a two-run single to center field, the final blow in his World Series MVP performance. Freeman's 12 RBIs in the five-game series tied Bobby Richardson for the World Series record. Richardson's dozen came in a seven-game series for the Yankees in 1960.

Teoscar Hernández capped the five-run inning with a two-run double that tied the game. All five runs in the inning scored after there were two outs. All five runs were unearned.

"We just took advantage of every mistake they made in that inning," Teoscar Hernández said. "We put some good at-bats together. We put the ball in play."

The Yankees did regain the lead with a run in the sixth inning. But the Dodgers mixed a broken-bat single, a walk, a catcher's interference call, and two sacrifice flies to take a 7–6 lead in the eighth.

But how would they close it out?

One of their high-leverage relievers, Evan Phillips, had to be left off the World Series roster with a sore shoulder, and Flaherty's early exit had forced Roberts into his bullpen earlier than planned.

When Brusdar Graterol ran into trouble in the sixth, Roberts pulled him for Blake Treinen, his most trusted reliever over the final two months or more of the season. His manager leaned on him like never before this time.

Treinen got Volpe to ground out to end the sixth, then retired the side in order in the seventh—and went back out for the eighth. Judge doubled with one out and Treinen walked Chisholm. Roberts went out to the mound.

Treinen had thrown 37 pitches already.

"I looked in his eyes," said Roberts, who could be seen placing a hand on Treinen's chest. "I said, 'How you feeling? How much more you got?'

"He said, 'I want it.' I trust him."

Like seemingly all of Roberts' decisions in the 2024 postseason, leaving his reliever in was the right one. Treinen got Giancarlo Stanton to fly out and struck out Anthony Rizzo, stranding two runners on base.

The 2⅓ innings were Treinen's longest outing since he went three innings for the Oakland A's on April 18, 2018. The 42 pitches were the most he had thrown since a 43-pitch, two-inning appearance for the A's in a 2018 postseason game against the Yankees.

And the Dodgers still had an inning to cover.

Early in the day, Game 3 starter Walker Buehler had crossed paths with Andrew Friedman in the Dodgers' clubhouse and told Friedman he wasn't going to throw his usual between-starts bullpen session before the game, in order to be available to pitch out of the bullpen if needed.

"'Yeah, yeah, Walker. That's great,'" Friedman recalled later, humoring Buehler, who would have been the Dodgers' Game 7 starter in a worst-case scenario. "'But what if things get wonky?'

[Buehler said.] 'Yeah, yeah—if things get wonky, no problem,' knowing that we had a fully rested bullpen. 'Yeah, yeah, yeah.'"

A few hours later, the Dodgers had fallen behind 5–0 after three innings and their starter had lasted just 1⅓. Friedman and his staff were trying to figure out how to get the team's Game 6 starter, Yoshinobu Yamamoto, a "lay-down" seat on a flight to Los Angeles as soon as possible, to maximize his rest before Game 6.

"As the [fifth] inning is unfolding, we go into the sixth. Walker comes in and says, 'Is this the definition of wonky?'" Friedman said, smiling broadly after the game. "'Yes, it is.'"

So it was Walker Buehler—he of the 1–6 record and 5.38 ERA during the regular season—who took the mound for the ninth inning at Yankee Stadium, looking to close out the Dodgers' first full-season championship since 1988.

He closed it out emphatically, getting Volpe to ground out, then striking out Austin Wells and Alex Verdugo. It was Buehler's 13th consecutive scoreless inning since his defense had broken down around him in the second inning of Game 3 of the NLDS. In four World Series appearances—starts in 2018, 2020, and 2024, and the 2024 closeout—Buehler allowed just one run in 19 innings.

"There were 30 other guys on this team that would have taken that inning," Buehler said. "I was just in the right spot."

The Dodgers put him there with their five-run comeback, the largest ever in a World Series–clinching victory.

"This game was no different than our entire season," Max Muncy said. "Get dealt a couple blows, come back from it. Get dealt some more blows, come back from it. This game was literally our season in a nutshell."

Shohei Ohtani finished his first postseason with a .230 average (14-for-61), three home runs, 10 RBIs, and 14 runs scored. Playing with an injured shoulder, he was just 2-for-19 in the World Series.

That shoulder injury proved to be more serious than Ohtani or the Dodgers let on during the Series. Just days after the Dodgers' victory parade through Los Angeles, Ohtani underwent arthroscopic surgery to repair a torn labrum.

The surgery on the back shoulder in his swing is not expected to impact Ohtani offensively next year, nor his return to pitching—though that will likely be delayed.

By putting off the completion of his rehab from the 2023 Tommy John surgery until after the Dodgers' 2024 postseason run, the team was already prepared for Ohtani's debut in their rotation to come at some point after the start of the 2025 schedule. The surgery on his non-throwing shoulder made it almost certain that Ohtani wouldn't be ready to pitch out of the gate in 2025—meaning he wouldn't start one of the games at the Tokyo Dome against the Chicago Cubs, in March 2025.

"We're just going to make sure we're checking every box to make sure he's in the best possible position health-wise," GM Brandon Gomes said. "And then whatever falls out of that smart, methodical process will be what it is.

"We're going to take it piece by piece and get through this… and not say, 'Hey, we need to be ready by this day.'"

None of that was on anyone's mind in the victorious clubhouse after the Dodgers became World Series champions. Emerging for an on-field interview, Ohtani said he had enjoyed each of the champagne celebrations along the way but had not indulged in the cigar smoking many of the Dodgers had made a stinky part of the tradition.

The 2024 victory, though, had filled in the last blank on Ohtani's résumé as a player.

"I think there is a legitimate argument that he is the greatest player to ever play this game," Dodgers president of baseball operations Andrew Friedman said, having successfully parlayed signing Ohtani into a World Series championship in the first year of his unprecedented 10-year contract. "Obviously, all this does is help further that.

"Seeing him tonight, celebrating, he said, 'Alright—nine more!' In his first year, we won a championship, so he thinks this is easy. We'll just do this nine more times."

It had been 36 years since Los Angeles hosted a parade for the Dodgers. The pandemic made it impossible after their 2020 championship. A crowd estimated at 250,000 filled downtown streets this time, and another 42,438 rocked Dodger Stadium for a post-parade victory rally featuring Ice Cube performing as Dave Roberts served as backup dancer.

One of the biggest roars of the rally came when Shohei Ohtani, prompted by Roberts, took the microphone and addressed the crowd in English.

"This is such a special moment for me," he said. "I'm so honored to be here and to be part of this team. Congratulations, Los Angeles. Thank you, fans."

Eleven months after signing Shohei Ohtani to the largest contract in professional sports history and topping $1 billion in salary commitments to new players, the Dodgers had cashed in with the (full-season) World Series championship that had eluded them despite their 12-year run of regular-season success.

If the Dodgers seemed to have gone all in to win a World Series in 2024, so be it, team president Stan Kasten said. They intended to go all in "next year and the next nine years after that."

"We're the Dodgers, Bill," Kasten told me in his office at Dodger Stadium before a game in midseason. "We brought this on ourselves. We are making no apologies for it. I've been in places where there are no expectations. This is better. It just is.

"I said it 12 years ago [when Guggenheim took over ownership of the Dodgers], we were going to go big or go home, and we're not going home. This is going to sound Pollyanna-ish but I believe it. We have had extraordinary support from this community, from this fan base—as they have supported it for decades. But it's because we support them too. We support them by what we put out there on the field. We invest in them. We invest in what we do for them in the stadium. We invest in them in what we do for the community—which is why they keep investing in us. It's a virtuous cycle that's a win-win for everybody.

"If we were taking a lot of money and putting it in our pockets and not putting a product out there, you could make a case. But that's not who we are. So, yeah, it's kind of a high-wire act. We need to spend a lot out there to drive the revenues we need. And let me tell you—in this sport you're competing against 29 other teams of really smart, committed, passionate people...And yet, here we are 12 years into this run of being a contending team. That's okay. We wouldn't have it any other way."

Epilogue

MVP x 3

When the Los Angeles Dodgers signed Shohei Ohtani to the largest contract ever given to a professional athlete, it created massive expectations for the team as a whole and Ohtani as an individual.

The team met them by winning the World Series. And Ohtani exceeded them with an unprecedented 50-50 season.

A two-time American League Most Valuable Player as a two-way player, Ohtani was voted the National League's Most Valuable Player for the historic season he put up as a designated hitter in 2024. The first 50-50 season in baseball history was enough to make him a unanimous MVP for a third time.

No other player has been voted MVP unanimously more than once.

"Obviously, I had moved to a new league and everything has been kind of a new experience," Ohtani said after the announcement. "There are so many great players in the National League, obviously. To be able to win the award unanimously is a great feeling. I'm very proud of that. Hopefully, I can continue in the upcoming seasons to be able to perform to this level."

By adding a National League MVP Award in his first season as a Dodger to his two American League MVP Awards with the Angels (2021 and 2023), Ohtani joined Hall of Famer Frank Robinson as the only players to win MVP awards in both leagues. Robinson won the NL MVP with the Cincinnati Reds in 1961 and the AL MVP with the Baltimore Orioles in 1966.

All of that—and a World Series championship in his first postseason.

"I think this is the 100 percent outcome with Shohei," Dodgers manager Dave Roberts said. "That's just speaking on the field, in the clubhouse. I can't imagine what he's doing outside of the game, on the business side.

"But as far as the baseball, between the lines, I just couldn't have imagined any better season."

No one could.

When Ohtani became a free agent following the 2023 season, the Dodgers knew they wanted to sign him. As part of their preparation, they tried to put a value on what adding a player as uniquely skilled as Ohtani would mean to a team.

"Certainly, what he's doing on the field this year alone, never mind when he actually comes back and pitches, I definitely think that somehow, someway, Shohei is underrated—which is wild, because he is capable of doing this offensively, and then you add legitimately one of the best starting pitchers also without actually having to add a pitcher," GM Brandon Gomes said from a distance deep into the 2024 season.

"We've tried to do it and tried to figure it out and I don't think it's accurately capturing how his value, how much there is to the team just on the field."

Off the field, Ohtani's impact on the Dodgers' business—his "value" to the team's bottom line—went beyond the Dodgers' wildest dreams.

"You ask me, 'Has it lived up to expectations?'" Dodgers team president and CEO Stan Kasten said in midseason. "No—it's way beyond anything before. Way beyond.

"Business-wise, without giving you numbers…it's blown away any projections we could have had."

So the record $700 million contract with its deferred money managed to be a bargain for the Dodgers—off the field, where it took their revenues to new heights, and on the field, where Ohtani performed historically.

Former Dodgers slugger Matt Kemp joked that, stripped of his pitching contributions for the year, Ohtani simply thought, "Oh, I can't pitch—I'll just hit 50 [home runs]."

While he denied setting any specific goals, Ohtani acknowledged that "the fact that I knew I wasn't going to be able to pitch this season just made me focus more on my offensive game."

That focus produced created a 50-50 club of one before going on to win the World Series title both he and the Dodgers craved.

"It was definitely special because we were able to win the World Series," Ohtani said, calling the honor "humbling."

"It will be a special moment that I will never forget, just to be able to win MVP as an individual as well. But I take it as a team effort, and this will motivate me more to win again next year."

Exceeding 2024 will not be easy. There have been very few better offensive seasons in MLB history.

Ohtani finished second in the majors in home runs (54, behind Aaron Judge's 58) and second in the majors in stolen bases (59, behind only Elly De La Cruz's 67). No player has finished in the top two of both of those categories since Ty Cobb, in 1909.

The 48th player to have a 30-30 season, Ohtani went on to become the fastest to 40-40 of the six players in that club, and he didn't stop until he had crashed through 50-50.

He led the National League in runs scored, RBIs, on-base percentage, slugging percentage, OPS, and home runs.

And he did all of that while rehabbing from the Tommy John surgery he underwent in September 2023.

Even his peers were in awe.

AL MVP Aaron Judge called Ohtani "the best player in the game."

Former MVP Mookie Betts said, "He's the best player on the field every day."

That was true in 2024 even though he spent less time on the field than anyone.

"I always thought that [a DH shouldn't win the MVP award]," Dodgers teammate (and 2020 NL MVP) Freddie Freeman said. "But the things he's doing this year, it's hard to argue against it.

"I've always thought it would be hard for a DH to win. He's only out there for four or five at-bats. But when you can potentially go 50-50, we might have to re-think that."

Voters agreed and made Ohtani the first full-time DH to win an MVP award. Prior to 2024, full-time DHs had finished as high as second in MVP voting four times. Boston's David Ortiz was the closest to winning, in 2005. He received 11 first-place votes and finished second to New York's Alex Rodriguez, who received 16 first-place votes.

"If he stole 50 bags, he probably would have won it," Betts (AL MVP 2018) joked of Ortiz, who hit .300 with 47 home runs and 148 RBIs—but stole just one base.

Ohtani is expected to return to two-way play in 2025, though the shoulder surgery he underwent following the World Series will likely delay his pitching debut for the Dodgers.

"The goal is to be ready for Opening Day. That includes hitting and pitching," Ohtani said in November 2024. "We are kind of taking our time. Obviously we want to make sure that I'm healthy first. We're not going to rush anything.

"I think we are going to take a little bit more time and be conservative and we're going to make sure I'm healthy before I step back on the mound."

The Dodgers are likely to limit Ohtani's innings in his first season back following a second Tommy John surgery. A late start to his pitching season would make that easier—and allow them to push more work later into the season, saving innings for another deep October run.

That will be the expectation of the reigning World Series champions. And the pressure for Ohtani to perform at historic levels will continue.

"I think of it as more of a blessing than pressure," Ohtani said in a Fox interview during the 2024 World Series. "Many fans tell me they came all the way from Japan to see me. I take that as a blessing and want to show them my best."

Acknowledgments

I've read books my whole life. Never thought I would write one.

But Shohei Ohtani has a way of changing everything in his wake, and his move from the Angels to the Dodgers created new opportunities for many—myself included.

My colleague with the Southern California Newspapers Group, Jeff Fletcher, had chronicled the first six years of Ohtani's MLB career as the Angels beat writer for SCNG and in two books (*Sho-Time* and *Sho-Time 2.0*).

When a Japanese publisher came to him interested in a third book, telling the story of Ohtani's move to the Dodgers, Jeff was kind enough to point them up the road to me. A project was born that I could not have handled without a great deal of help.

Thank you first of all to Jud Laghi, who guided me through the publishing world, finding a U.S. partner in Triumph Books.

Juggling my daily responsibilities as a beat writer covering the Dodgers during this historic season while also building a book that would tell the whole story was not easy. Thank you to the Dodgers' media relations staff (Joe Jareck, Juan Dorado, and Ally Salvage) for their help, patience, and not calling the police on me.

I owe a great deal of gratitude to my constant companions on the beat, fellow members of the "Core Four"—Jack Harris of the *Los Angeles Times*, Fabian Ardaya of The Athletic, and Juan Toribio of MLB.com—for their support, camaraderie, and tolerance of the old guy on the beat. The same goes to my *tomodachi* in the Japanese press, who made the unique challenge of covering one of the most popular athletes on the planet enjoyable.

So many members of the Dodgers' organization were generous with their time, most prominently Dodgers manager Dave Roberts, who is as accessible and patient as any manager I have covered. I'm grateful to him and his coaching staff, as well as to Stan Kasten, Andrew Friedman, Brandon Gomes, Brandon McDaniel, Galen Carr, and Lon Rosen, for their generosity with their time.

A special thank-you to my youngest son, Alex, who found himself doing a lot more yard work over the past year while Dad was working on this book. I'll learn how to use the lawn mower again now, Alex.

Finally, I am grateful to Tom Moore and Todd Bailey of SCNG for, well, allowing me to stay employed throughout this process.

Sources

The majority of the material in this book came from interviews I conducted myself or was present for. But there were a number of additional sources on which I relied:

Anderson, R.J. "Baseball Gambling Scandals: Padres' Tucupita Marcano Joins Shohei Ohtani's Interpreter, Pete Rose, Black Sox," CBS Sports, June 4, 2024.

Apstein, Stephanie. "Shohei Ohtani Strives to Be the Absolute Best…Even at Getting Some Shuteye," *Sports Illustrated*, March 15, 2024.

Apstein, Stephanie. "New Dodgers Shohei Ohtani, Teoscar Hernández Aren't Letting Language Barriers Get in the Way," *Sports Illustrated*, April 29, 2024.

Asinof, Eliot. *Eight Men Out: The Black Sox and the 1919 World Series*, Holt Rinehart & Winston, 1963.

Baer, Jack. "Shohei Ohtani Reportedly Buys $7.85 million Los Angeles Mansion from Adam Carolla," Yahoo! Sports, May 22, 2024.

Bloom, Barry M. "MLB's Rules on Gambling: What Happens When Players Bet?" Sportico, June 14, 2024.

Blum, Sam. "This Fan Caught Shohei Ohtani's First Home Run as a Dodger; Hard Feelings Ensued," The Athletic, April 4, 2024.

Carroll, Will. "Dr. Frank Jobe, Tommy John and the Surgery That Changed Baseball Forever," Bleacher Report, July 17, 2023.

Cohen, Jay. "50 Years Later, Tommy John Surgery Remains a Game-Changer," Associated Press, March 13, 2024.

DiGiovanna, Mike. "Dodgers Supportive of Shohei Ohtani: 'Betrayal Is Hard,'" *Los Angeles Times*, March 26, 2024.

Farmer, Sam. "Should Shohei Ohtani Pitch in the Playoffs? Neal ElAttrache, His Surgeon, Has Thoughts," *Los Angeles Times*, September 27, 2024.

Harris, Jack. "Shohei Ohtani's Three-Run Blast Caps Memorable All-Star Week for Dodgers," *Los Angeles Times*, July 16, 2024.

Harris, Jack. "Shohei Ohtani's Labrum Surgery Could Delay Return to Pitching but Shouldn't Impact Swing," *Los Angeles Times*, November 7, 2024.

Larsen, Peter. "Shohei Ohtani's Ex-Interpreter Linked to 'Real Housewives of Orange County' Star," *Orange County Register*, May 8, 2024.

McCullough, Andy. "Dodgers Believe Pitch to Ohtani Was Waste High," *Los Angeles Times*, March 8, 2018.

Nightengale, Bob. "Shohei Ohtani's Agent Provides Inside Look at Historic Contract Negotiations," *USA Today*, December 15, 2023.

Nightengale, Bob. "Dodgers Provide Preview of Next Decade as Shohei Ohtani, Yoshinobu Yamamoto Play Together," *USA Today*, March 6, 2024.

Osborne, Cary. "Dodgers Introduce Players to Their Brand New Lab," Dodger Insider, March 4, 2024.

Saavedra, Tony. "California Bookie at Center of Gambling Scandal," *Orange County Register*, March 28, 2024.

Sunkara, Bhaskar, "The Legalization of Sports Gambling in the US Was a Mistake," *The Guardian*, April 22, 2024.

Saitō, Nobuhiro. "Unmasking Shohei Ohtani's Interpreter Mizuhara Ippei," Nippon.com, October 11, 2021.

Thompson, Tisha. "Dodgers Fire Shohei Ohtani's Interpreter Amid Allegations of 'Massive Theft,'" ESPN.com, March 20, 2024.

"Sound Sleep Helping Shohei Ohtani Achieve His Two-Way Baseball Dreams," Kyodo News, October 19, 2022.

"Full Translation of Shohei Ohtani's Statement on Ippei Mizuhara Gambling Scandal," The Mainichi, March 26, 2024.